SAUDI ARABIA
AND
YEMEN

MIDDLE EAST

REGION IN TRANSITION

SAUDI ARABIA AND YEMEN

Edited by Laura S. Etheredge, Associate Editor, Middle East Geography

Britannica Educational Publishing

in association with

ROSEN EDUCATIONAL SERVICES

Published in 2011 by Britannica Educational Publishing
(a trademark of Encyclopædia Britannica, Inc.)
in association with Rosen Educational Services, LLC
29 East 21st Street, New York, NY 10010.

Distributed exclusively by Rosen Educational Services.
For a listing of additional Britannica Educational Publishing titles, call toll free (800) 237-9932.

First Edition

Britannica Educational Publishing
Michael I. Levy: Executive Editor
J.E. Luebering: Senior Manager
Marilyn L. Barton: Senior Coordinator, Production Control
Steven Bosco: Director, Editorial Technologies
Lisa S. Braucher: Senior Producer and Data Editor
Yvette Charboneau: Senior Copy Editor
Kathy Nakamura: Manager, Media Acquisition
Laura S. Etheredge: Associate Editor, Middle East Geography

Rosen Educational Services
Jeanne Nagle: Editor
Nelson Sá: Art Director
Cindy Reiman: Photography Manager
Matthew Cauli: Designer, Cover Design
Introduction by Laura Loria

Library of Congress Cataloging-in-Publication Data

Saudi Arabia and Yemen / edited by Laura S. Etheredge.

p. cm. — (Middle East : region in transition)
"In association with Britannica Educational Publishing, Rosen Educational Services."
Includes bibliographical references and index.
ISBN 978-1-61530-335-9 (library binding)
1. Saudi Arabia. 2. Saudi Arabia—History. 3. Saudi Arabia—Politics and government. 4. Saudi Arabia—Social conditions. 5. Social change—Saudi Arabia—History. 6. Yemen (Republic) 7. Yemen (Republic)—History. 8. Yemen (Republic—Politics and government. 9. Yemen (Republic)—Social conditions. 10. Social change—Yemen (Republic)—History. I. Etheredge, Laura.
DS204.S3123 2011
953.8—dc22

2010026863

Manufactured in the United States of America

On the cover: Clockwise from upper left: The spire of the modern Kingdom Centre tower and an ancient minaret, Riyadh, Saudi Arabia; a view of the city of Sanaa showing traditional Yemeni architecture; coffee seller in the Old Town section of Sanaa, Yemen; Al-Dirʿiyyah, the former capital of Saudi Arabia *Ian Cumming/Axiom Photographic Agency/Getty Images; Shutterstock.com; Bruno Morandi/The Image Bank/Getty Images; Shutterstock.com*

On pages 1, 14, 26, 36, 44, 74, 86, 100, 108, 117, 144, 146, 152: Stone and brick houses line a street and seem to flank a distant minaret, in the Yemeni city of Sanaa. *Thomas J. Abercrombie/National Geographic/Getty Images*

CONTENTS

34

43

63

79

101

105

118

139

INTRODUCTION

The Middle East hosts a great diversity of people and political systems. This volume focuses on Saudi Arabia and Yemen—two countries on the Arabian Peninsula with some shared history based on economic interdependence, political interrelationship, and historically fluid borders. This book takes an in-depth look at these countries' unique cultures, political systems, and state of affairs, past and present.

Saudi Arabia dominates the Arabian Peninsula, four-fifths of which lies within that country alone. Yemen, which lies to the south of Saudi Arabia on the peninsula, is far smaller. Both countries share a border with Oman and, to the west, are bordered by the Red Sea. Deserts dominate the interior of Saudi Arabia and north and northeastern Yemen, and both countries are virtually devoid of permanent waterways. The arid climate and poor soil conditions limit agricultural productivity, though less so in Yemeni highlands, where fruit, grains, coffee, and khat, a mild stimulant popular in Yemeni culture, are raised.

Ethnically, the people of the Arabian Peninsula are predominantly Arab, but a variety of tribal affiliations subdivide these countries. In Yemen, there is a further divide between northern and southern groups that frames the social and political organization of the country. Saudi Arabia also has a history of tribal affiliation, but has also experienced a greater influx of visitors and workers from surrounding countries. Arabic is the dominant language of the region, spoken in a variety of different dialects. Sunni Islam predominates in both states, although Yemen adheres to the Shāfiʿī school of jurisprudence and Saudi Arabia has been influenced by the Wahhābī movement,

Illustration of an ancient pilgrim caravan as it arrives in Mecca. Fotosearch/Archive Photos/Getty Images

which is a strict interpretation of the Ḥanbalī school. Minority groups of Shīʿite Muslims exist in both countries, but in Yemen they have historically succeeded in achieving political influence, particularly in the north, in the form of the Zaydī school.

Yemen 's largely rural population is, for the most part, evenly distributed. Villages, which are usually small, feature multi-storied homes in which families live in the upper floors and goods are kept below, providing a measure of security. Older parts of cities are walled, but newer homes for the wealthy are typically built in suburbs. Conversely, the majority of Saudi Arabians live in cities. Among the country's largest urban areas are the capital, Riyadh; Jiddah, a commercial center on the Red Sea; and Mecca and Medina, which have enormous religious significance.

Saudi Arabia is famous for its rich petroleum reserves, which are the dominant force in its economy. Though dependent on world oil prices, the country is one of the richest in the world thanks to these reserves. During the 1970s and '80s, the government gained control of Aramco, originally an oil enterprise of the United States, which brought in so much revenue that the country was virtually at full employment.

In contrast, Yemen is one of the poorest countries in the world. Oil reserves were first discovered in 1984, more than 40 years after they were discovered in Saudi Arabia. Exploration for oil and natural gas continues, but the sector is still yet to be fully developed. Many Yemeni men have traditionally emigrated for employment, especially to Saudi Arabia. However, political conflict between the two countries in the late 20th century has reversed the flow of workers northward, causing serious damage to the Yemeni economy.

In both Yemen and Saudi Arabia, all legislation and judicial decisions are based on the Sharīʿah, or Islamic law. That is where the political similarities end between the two states. Saudi Arabia is a monarchy and has no constitution. The king acts as the final authority in all matters executive, legislative, and judicial, although he may seek the advice of a Council of Ministers who serve at his pleasure. The kingdom is divided into regions, each headed by an appointed governor (who is usually a member of the royal family) who leads a council, half of whose members are elected. Tribal and religious leaders are influential in maintaining the local social order.

By contrast, the unification of North and South Yemen in 1990 produced a constitution that calls for elements of a democracy. The president, who is elected by popular vote, appoints the vice president, prime minister, and one of the two houses of the legislature; the other house also is elected. Local governorates, with a governor appointed by the president and elected councils, are meant to have a great deal of autonomy, although their elections are still susceptible to influence by the central government. Political parties are regulated and licensed by the government to limit tribal or ethnic influence.

The quality of life in these two states is radically different, chiefly because of their disparate levels of wealth. Yemen's health care system lacks monetary and human resources; many foreign aid agencies operate in Yemen to address health care needs. Housing is generally of poor quality, and most rural areas lack plumbing and electricity. The educational system also suffers from lack of money and teachers. The literacy rate ranges from more than three-fourths of men to around two-fifths of women, and very few Yemenis attend university. Those wealthy enough often send their children abroad to study.

In Saudi Arabia, a series of five-year plans, begun in the 1970s, have elevated the quality of life to Western standards. Hospitals and dispensaries serve the medical needs of the people, and more doctors are being trained locally rather than abroad. The government encourages the construction of modern housing with generous loan programs. Newer homes near cities have plumbing, electricity, and good telecommunications systems, although rural areas have not caught up yet. A sizable investment in education has yielded a high literacy rate in Saudi Arabia. Elementary, intermediate, and secondary schools focus on religious education, while universities also focus on science, technology, and medicine.

Both Saudi Arabia and Yemen have histories of occupation and influence by outside imperial powers. Modern Saudi Arabian history is linked to the Wahhābī religious movement. In the early 18th century, Muḥammad ibn ʿAbd al-Wahhāb aligned with the prince of Al-Dirʿiyyah, Muḥammad ibn Saʿūd, to conquer neighboring territories; his successors continued the expansion efforts. By the turn of the century, the Ottomans and British had begun to push back at Wahhābī forces. In this effort they enlisted Muḥammad ʿAlī, the virtually autonomous viceroy of Egypt, whose son Ṭūsūn captured Mecca and Medina in 1812; the Egyptian force succeeded in advancing into central Arabia a few years later. Ensuing battles resulted in the imprisonment of most of the Saʿūd family and many Wahhābī leaders. Although the Wahhābī empire itself was no more, its beliefs lived on in its followers.

The 1824 capture of the city of Riyadh by Turkī, the grandson of Muḥammad ibn Saʿūd, ushered in the second Saʿūdī state. Fayṣal, his son and successor, was significant in reestablishing Wahhābī dominance over the course of his rule, which extended, although once interrupted, from 1834 until his death in 1865. Fayṣal's sons quarreled over who was to succeed him. After several years of infighting, his eldest son, ʿAbd Allāh, turned to the Ottoman governor of Baghdad for help. Although the Ottoman governor assisted ʿAbd Allāh, at the same time he carved out a leadership role for himself and occupied Al-Hasa for 42 years. The Rashīdīs, a rival family from Ḥāʾil, fought for power as well, and took advantage of the Saʿūd family's internal struggle, battling for and winning control of the Wahhābī state in 1891.

The third Saʿūdī state was initiated when Ibn Saʿūd stormed Riyadh in 1902, reclaiming power for his family. A strategy of acknowledging the Ottomans and maintaining a cordial relationship with the British, all the while retaining rule over central Arabia, served Ibn Saʿūd well. He focused on internal organization and expanding his authority across the dual kingdoms of Najd and the Hejaz.

In 1927, Britain recognized the Saʿūdī state as independent under Ibn Saʿūd, who united his kingdom under the name Saudi Arabia in 1932. For the most part, the country was able to quickly demarcate its frontiers with Jordan, Iraq, and Kuwait; its border dispute with Yemen, however, would linger for decades thereafter. When it entered World War II against the Germans, Saudi Arabia gained entry into the United Nations. Under pressure from religious conservatives, Ibn Saʿūd was cautious of relations with neighboring Arab states, playing a minor role in the Arab League.

The discovery of oil reserves led to a huge increase in wealth for the kingdom. Aramco, founded in conjunction with U.S. interests, paid a large income tax to the state, and drew many foreign workers to Saudi Arabia. Saʿūd, the son and successor of Ibn Saʿūd, did not readily welcome the foreign influence. Conversely, his half-brother and eventual successor, Fayṣal, was experienced in foreign affairs and welcomed what he considered modernization. Saudi Arabia's greatest influence at the time came from the United States, and although the kingdom aligned itself with the United States during the Cold War, it was not in favor of U.S. support of Israel.

During the 1970s and '80s, Saudi Arabia gained full control of Aramco and, subsequently, worldwide dominance of the oil industry. During the Persian Gulf War of 1990-91, King Fahd hosted U.S. troops to protect Saudi Arabia and Kuwait. While the maneuver was successful, it led some groups, particularly Islamists, to question whether the royal family could protect its own kingdom from outside influence. A general sense of malaise simmered in the wake of the Gulf War. Fahd's response was to issue the Basic Law of Government in 1992, which guided how the Saudi government was to be run and outlined the rights and responsibilities of the country's citizens. Under Fahd's successor, 'Abd Allāh, further tentative reforms were undertaken.

Yemen also experienced a period of competing British and Ottoman rule throughout the 19th century. By 1904, a treaty between the two powers established a border between the Ottoman north and the British south, cementing the demarcation between two Yemens for most of the century. The north claimed its independence in 1918, and the Zaydī imam Yaḥyā Maḥmūd al-Mutawakkil became the country's de facto leader. Imam Yaḥyā clashed with the British in his attempt to wrest control of the south. Following his assassination, his son Aḥmad continued the dynasty with an oppressive reign.

A revolution in 1962 toppled Aḥmad's son shortly after his succession, spurring efforts by the south to shake

British rule. The conflict between Yemeni groups seeking to govern after independence mounted into open warfare, and in November 1967 Britain relinquished its power in the south. With two independent Yemens, unification seemed imminent, but their ideologies were too diverse for an easy merger. Over time, however, progress was made toward unification. Due to a destabilizing withdrawal of support by the Soviet Union for some of South Yemen's allies and the discovery of oil and natural gas reserves in both countries (and across territory disputed between them), the south was ready to unite. It was the northern regime of ʿAlī ʿAbd Allāh Ṣāliḥ, though, that initiated the push for unification. In 1990, each country's legislature voted to adopt a new, shared constitution, and unified Yemen was established as a multi-party democracy with its capital in the city of Sanaa and with Ṣāliḥ as interim president.

The Persian Gulf War and the subsequent collapse of Yemen's economy temporarily delayed planned elections for the newly unified country. Internal conflict in 1993–94 expanded into civil war mid-1994; unrest in the wake of the civil war concentrated power in the hands of President Ṣāliḥ and resulted in some curtailment of political freedoms. Economic difficulties continued to persist, and efforts to remedy the situation—particularly with the assistance of World Bank and International Monetary Fund initiatives—were ongoing into the 21st century.

In the 21st century, Yemen and Saudi Arabia were involved in the United States's "war on terror." Yemen's President Ṣāliḥ pledged to support the United States but had to balance his actions against a large faction of traditionalists who shunned outside interference. King Fahd of Saudi Arabia refused to support the U.S. war in Iraq, a move that seemed to some to be an attempt to appease radical Islamist factions within the kingdom. His successor,

'Abd Allāh, has not been as tolerant of extremists, and has enacted reforms regarding elections and deregulation.

Change is the only constant in the world, and Yemen and Saudi Arabia are no exceptions. As a developing nation, Yemen struggles to improve its security situation and to strengthen itself economically and politically. Saudi Arabia is working toward greater political participation for its citizens while maintaining a peaceful succession of royals. The relationship between Yemen and Saudi Arabia—and between each country and the West—remain important factors as each moves forward.

Saudi Arabia: The Land and Its People

CHAPTER 1

Saudi Arabia occupies about four-fifths of the Arabian Peninsula. It is bordered by Jordan, Iraq, and Kuwait to the north; the Persian Gulf, Qatar, the United Arab Emirates, and Oman to the east; Yemen to the south and southwest; and the Red Sea and the Gulf of Aqaba to the west. Long-running border disputes were resolved with Yemen (2000) and Qatar (2001), while the border with the United Arab Emirates remains undefined. A territory of 2,200 square miles (5,700 square kilometres [km]) along the gulf coast was shared by Kuwait and Saudi Arabia as a neutral zone until 1969, when a political boundary was

Saudi Arabia. Encyclopaedia Britannica, Inc.

agreed upon. Each of the two countries administers one-half of the territory, but they equally share oil production in the entire area. The controversy over the Saudi-Iraqi Neutral Zone was legally settled in 1981 by partition, yet conflict between the two countries persisted and prevented final demarcation on the ground.

Saudi Arabia, once a country of small cities and towns, has become increasingly urban. Traditional centres such as Jiddah, Mecca, and Medina have grown into large cities, and the capital, Riyadh, a former oasis town, has grown into a modern metropolis. Many of the region's traditional nomads, the Bedouin, have been settled in cities or agrarian communities. The sedentary population of the country views those few Bedouin who maintain the traditional desert lifestyle with deep ambivalence. They are, at the same time, the link to the country's past and its solid foundation.

RELIEF

The Arabian Peninsula is dominated by a plateau that rises abruptly from the Red Sea and dips gently toward the Persian Gulf. In the north, the western highlands are upward of 5,000 feet (1,500 metres [m]) above sea level, decreasing slightly to 4,000 feet (1,200 m) in the vicinity of Medina and increasing southeastward to more than 10,000 feet (3,000 m). Mount Sawdā', which is situated near Abhā in the south, is generally considered the highest point in the country. Estimates of its elevation range from 10,279 to 10,522 feet (3,133 to 3,207 m). The watershed of the peninsula is only 25 miles (40 km) from the Red Sea in the north and recedes to 80 miles (130 km) near the Yemen border. The coastal plain, known as the Tihāmah, is virtually nonexistent in the north, except for occasional wadi deltas, but it widens slightly toward the south. The imposing escarpment that runs parallel to the Red Sea is somewhat interrupted by a gap northwest of Mecca but becomes more clearly continuous to the south.

Toward the interior, the surface gradually descends into the broad plateau area of the Najd, which is covered with lava flows and volcanic debris as well as with occasional sand accumulations; it slopes down from an elevation of about 4,500 feet (1,370 m) in the west to about 2,500 feet (760 m) in the east. There the drainage is more clearly dendritic (i.e., branching) and is much more extensive than that flowing toward the Red Sea. To the east, this region is bounded by a series of long, low ridges, with steep slopes on the west and gentle slopes on the east; the area is 750 miles (1,200 km) long and curves eastward from north to south. The most prominent of the

The Rubʿ al-Khali, a massive desert lying mainly in southeastern Saudi Arabia, with lesser portions in Yemen, Oman, and the United Arab Emirates. Lynn Abercrombie

ridges are the Ṭuwayq Mountains (Jibāl Ṭuwayq), which rise from the plateau at an elevation of some 2,800 feet (850 m) above sea level and reach more than 3,500 feet (1,100 m) southwest of Riyadh, overlooking the plateau's surface to the west by 800 feet (250 m) and more.

The interior of the Arabian Peninsula contains extensive sand surfaces. Among them is the world's largest sand area, the Rubʿ al-Khali ("Empty Quarter"), which dominates the southern part of the country and covers more than 250,000 square miles (647,500 square km). It slopes from above 2,600 feet (800 m) near the border with Yemen northeastward down almost to sea level near the Persian Gulf; individual sand mountains reach elevations of 800 feet (250 m), especially in the eastern part. A smaller sand area of about 22,000 square miles (57,000 square km), called Al-Nafūd (*nafūd* designating a sandy area or desert), is in the north-central part of the country. A great arc of sand, Al-Dahnā', almost 900 miles (1,450 km) long but in places only 30 miles (50 km) wide, joins Al-Nafūd with the Rubʿ al-Khali. Eastward, as the plateau surface slopes very gradually down to the gulf, there are numerous salt flats (*sabkhah*s) and marshes. The gulf coastline is irregular, and the coastal waters are very shallow.

DRAINAGE AND SOILS

There are virtually no permanent surface streams in the country, but wadis are numerous. Those leading to the Red Sea are short and steep, though one unusually long extension is made by Wadi Al-Ḥamḍ, which rises near Medina and flows inland to the northwest for 100 miles (160 km) before turning westward. Those draining eastward are longer and more developed except in Al-Nafūd and the Rubʿ al-Khali. Soils are poorly developed. Large areas are covered with pebbles of varying sizes. Alluvial deposits are found in wadis, basins, and oases. Salt flats are especially common in the east.

CLIMATE

There are three climatic zones in the kingdom: (1) desert almost everywhere, (2) steppe along the western highlands, forming a strip less than 100 miles (160 km) wide in the north but becoming almost 300 miles (480 km) wide at the latitude of Mecca, and (3) a small area of humid and mild temperature conditions, with long summers, in the highlands just north of Yemen.

In winter, cyclonic weather systems generally skirt north of the Arabian Peninsula, moving eastward from the Mediterranean Sea, though sometimes they reach eastern and central Arabia and the Persian Gulf. Some weather systems move southward along the Red Sea trough and provide winter precipitation as far south as Mecca and sometimes as far as Yemen. In March and April, some precipitation, normally torrential, falls. In summer, the highlands of Asir (ʿAsīr), southeast of Mecca, receive enough precipitation from the monsoonal winds to support a steppelike strip of land.

Winters, from December to February, are cool, and frost and snow may occur in the southern highlands. Average temperatures for the coolest months, December through February, are in the mid-70s F (low 20s C) at Jiddah, high 50s F (mid-10s C) at Riyadh, and low 60s F (high 10s C) at Al-Dammām. Summers, from June to August, are hot, with daytime temperatures in the shade exceeding 100 °F (38 °C) in almost all of the country. Temperatures in the desert frequently rise as high as 130 °F (55 °C) in the summer. Humidity is low, except along the coasts, where it can be high and very oppressive. The level of precipitation is also low throughout the country, amounting to about 2.5 inches (65 mm) at Jiddah, a little more than 3 inches (75 mm) at Riyadh, and 3 inches at Al-Dammām. These figures, however, represent mean annual precipitation, and large variations are normal. In the highlands of Asir, more than 19 inches (480 mm) a year may be received, falling mostly between May and October when the summer monsoon winds prevail. In the Rubʿ al-Khali, a decade may pass with no precipitation at all.

PLANT AND ANIMAL LIFE

Much of Saudi Arabia's vegetation belongs to the North African–Indian desert region. Plants are xerophytic (requiring little water) and are mostly small herbs and shrubs that are useful as forage. There are a few small areas of grass and trees in southern Asir. Although the date

Bedouin woman with Arabian camels (dromedaries) near Madāʾin Ṣāliḥ, Saudi Arabia. Lynn Abercrombie

palm (*Phoenix dactylifera*) is widespread, about one-third of the date palms grown are in Al-Sharqiyyah province.

Animal life includes wolves, hyenas, foxes, honey badgers, mongooses, porcupines, baboons, hedgehogs, hares, sand rats, and jerboas. Larger animals such as gazelles, oryx, leopards, and mountain goats were relatively numerous until about 1950, when hunting from motor vehicles reduced these animals almost to extinction. Birds include falcons (which are caught and trained for hunting), eagles, hawks, vultures, owls, ravens, flamingos, egrets, pelicans, doves, and quail, as well as sand grouse and bulbuls. There are several species of snakes, many of which are poisonous, and numerous types of lizards. There is a wide variety of marine life in the gulf. Domesticated animals include camels, fat-tailed sheep, long-eared goats, salukis, donkeys, and chickens.

ETHNIC GROUPS

Although the country's tribes are often considered "pure" Arabs—certainly they are the descendants of the peninsula's original ethnic populations—a certain degree of ethnic heterogeneity is evident among both the sedentary and nomadic populations of Saudi Arabia. Variations have developed because of a long history of regionalism and tribal autonomy and because some localities have been subjected to important outside influences. Thus, the proximity of sub-Saharan Africa along the Red Sea littoral and the constant historical influx of peoples from Iran, Pakistan, and India along the Persian Gulf coast have left traces of the physical types characteristic of those peoples among the native population. Likewise, the hajj (pilgrimage) to Mecca has long brought hundreds of thousands of people annually from various ethnic groups to the country. About half of all pilgrims travel from Arab countries and half from African and Asian countries. A small number of such visitors have settled in and around the holy cities throughout the years, either out of religious devotion or because penury prevented their return home.

Since the 1960s, an increasing number of outsiders have entered and left Saudi Arabia. By the early 21st century, the estimated number of foreign workers was between one-fourth and one-fifth of the country's total population, in spite of efforts by the Saudi authorities to encourage citizens to occupy positions typically held by foreigners. At first, most expatriated workers were Arab, such as Yemenis, Egyptians, Palestinians, Syrians, and Iraqis. Increasing numbers of non-Arab Muslims such as Pakistanis have been employed, as have large numbers of non-Muslim Koreans and Filipinos, who have been hired under group contracts for specified periods. Most specialized technical workers are Europeans and Americans.

LANGUAGES

Arabic is a Semitic language of numerous vernacular dialects that originated on the Arabian Peninsula. There are three main dialect groups in Saudi Arabia—in the eastern, central, and western parts of the country—though these are not always clearly discernible from one another because of the pervasiveness of local variations. There are various degrees of mutual intelligibility among dialect groups, but some differences are quiet pronounced. The written language, Modern Standard Arabic, is derived from Classical Arabic, the language of the Qur'ān, and is used as a literary koine within the kingdom and throughout the broader Arab world. Various dialects of Arabic from other regions are also spoken by expatriate workers, as are numerous other non-Arabic languages such as Persian, Urdu, Pashto, Tagalog, and Korean. English is widely understood.

RELIGION

Saudi Arabia is the birthplace of Islam, and most of its natives are adherents of the majority Sunni branch. In modern times, the Wahhābī interpretation of Sunni Islam has been especially influential, and Muslim scholars espousing that sect's views have been a major social and political force. Wahhābism, as it is called in the West (members refer to themselves as *muwaḥḥidūn*, "unitarians"), is a strict interpretation of the Ḥanbalī school of Islamic jurisprudence and is named for Muḥammad ibn ʿAbd al-Wahhāb (1703–92), a religious scholar whose alliance with Ibn Saʿūd led to the establishment of the first Saʿūdī state. The current government of Saudi Arabia (i.e., the Saʿūd family) has largely relied on religion—including its close and continuing ties to Wahhābism and its status as the custodian of Mecca and Medina, the two holy cities of Islam—to establish its political legitimacy. The king is supposed to uphold Islam and apply its precepts and, in turn, is subject to its constraints. But at times he and the royal family have come under criticism for failing to do so.

Shīʿites, adherents of the second major branch of Islam, make up a small portion of the population and are found mostly in the oases of Al-Hasa and Al-Qaṭīf in the eastern part of the country. Most are of the Ithnā ʿAsharī, or Twelver branch, although there remain small numbers of Ismāʿīlīs. The only Christians are foreign workers and businessmen. The country's once small Jewish population is now apparently extinct. Other religions are practiced among foreign workers. Public worship and display by non-Muslim faiths is prohibited. Public displays by non-Wahhābī Muslim groups, including by other Sunni sects, have been limited and even banned by the government. Sufism, for instance, is not openly practiced, nor is celebration of the Prophet's birthday (*mawlid*). Shīʿites have suffered the greatest persecution.

SETTLEMENT PATTERNS

Four traditional regions stand out—the Hejaz, Asir, Najd, and Al-Hasa (transliterated more precisely as Al-Ḥijāz, ʾAsīr, Najd, and Al-Aḥsāʾ, respectively). The Hejaz, in the northwest, contains Mecca and Medina, as well as one of the kingdom's primary ports, Jiddah. Asir is the highland region south of the Hejaz; its capital, Abhā, lies at an elevation of about 8,000 feet (2,400 m). Subregions in Asir are formed by the oasis cluster of Najrān—a highland area north of Yemen—and by the coastal plain, the Tihāmah. Najd occupies a large part of the interior and includes the capital, Riyadh. Al-Hasa, in the east along the Persian Gulf, includes the principal petroleum-producing areas.

Nomadism, the form of land use with which the kingdom is traditionally associated, has become virtually nonexistent, and the pattern of extensive land use traditionally practiced by the nomadic Bedouin has been supplanted by the highly intensive patterns of urban land use. More than four-fifths of Saudi Arabia's total population live in cities, and almost all of the rest live in government-supported agricultural enterprises.

The major areas of population are in the central Hejaz, in Asir, in central Najd, and near the Persian Gulf. The largest towns are cosmopolitan in character, and some are associated with dominant functions: Mecca and Medina are religious, Riyadh is political and administrative, and Jiddah is commercial. Dhahran (Al-Ẓahrān), near the Persian Gulf coast in Al-Sharqiyyah province, is the administrative centre of Saudi Aramco (Arabian American Oil Company), and nearby Al-Khubar and Al-Dammām are important commercial coastal towns. Al-Jubayl on the

Thousands of worshipers gather at Mecca's Ḥaram Mosque (Great Mosque) at sunset during Ramadan. AFP/Getty Images

Gulf and Yanbuʿ on the Red Sea are the terminus points of oil and gas pipelines, and large petrochemical industrial complexes are located in both. Other large cities include Al-Ṭāʾif, Al-Hufūf, Tabūk, Buraydah, Al-Mubarraz, Khamīs Mushayṭ, Najrān, Ḥāʾil, Jīzān, and Abhā.

DEMOGRAPHIC TRENDS

A major demographic theme since the early 20th century has been the government's policy of settling the Bedouin. This practice has largely been successful, though sedentary Bedouin remain strongly attached to their tribal affiliation. A second major theme has been an influx of foreign workers (first foreign Arabs and later workers from other regions) since the 1950s. No exact numbers are available, but it is generally agreed that these foreign workers have numbered in the millions. Some Arabs, particularly early arrivals, have been naturalized, but most are temporary, albeit often long-term, residents. Moreover, most of these are unaccompanied males who have left their families in their native land; this situation is particularly true for lower-paid workers. Although large numbers of Saudi citizens travel abroad for school or holiday, the number of those settling abroad is relatively small.

Thanks partly to the government's policies promoting large families and partly to its large investment in health care, the country's birth rate is well above the world average. The national death rate is markedly below the world standard. As a result, Saudi Arabia's overall rate of natural increase is significantly higher than the world average, and its population is extremely young, with roughly two-thirds under 30 years old and about one-third younger than 15. Life expectancy averages about 70 years for men and about 75 years for women.

Jiddah

Jiddah (also spelled Jidda or Jeddah) is a city and major port in central Hejaz region in western Saudi Arabia. It lies along the Red Sea west of Mecca. The principal importance of Jiddah in history is that it constituted the port of Mecca and was thus the site where the majority of Muslim pilgrims landed who were journeying to the holy cities of Mecca and Medina. The city in fact owes its commercial foundations to the caliph ʿUthmān, who in 646 made it the port for Muslim pilgrims crossing the Red Sea. In 1916 Jiddah and its Turkish garrisons surrendered to British forces. It then formed part of the Kingdom of the Hejaz until 1925, when it was captured by Ibn Saʿūd. In the 1927 Treaty of Jiddah the British recognized Saudi sovereignty over the Hejaz and Najd regions. Jiddah eventually was incorporated into Saudi Arabia. In 1947 the city walls were demolished, and rapid expansion followed. The city takes its name (which means "ancestress," or "grandmother") from the location there of the reputed tomb of Eve, which was destroyed by the Saudi government in 1928 in the belief that it encouraged superstition.

After World War II, Jiddah was completely modernized and expanded with the new wealth acquired by Saudi Arabia from oil royalties. Its harbour was deepened and enlarged to accommodate large vessels, and a desalinization plant was constructed in the early 1970s, thought to be the largest in the world at its completion. The city's economy, once dependent on pilgrim expenditures and fishing, was diversified to include steel-rolling mills, oil refineries, and the manufacture of cement, clothing, and pottery. Other activities include cattle raising and dairying and many small industries. One of Saudi Arabia's largest cities and busiest seaports, Jiddah was the diplomatic capital of the country and the location of the Saudi ministry of foreign affairs and of the embassies and missions of foreign governments before these were all transferred to the Saudi capital of Riyadh in the mid-1980s. Advanced education in economics and administration is offered by King Abdulaziz University, founded in 1967. Jiddah is served by highways to Mecca and Medina and by King Abdulaziz International Airport.

CHAPTER 2

The Saudi Arabian Economy

Fueled by enormous revenues from oil exports, the economy boomed during the 1970s and '80s. Unlike most developing countries, Saudi Arabia had an abundance of capital, and vast development projects sprung up that turned the once underdeveloped country into a modern state. During that time, unemployment was all but nonexistent—large numbers of foreign workers were imported to do the most menial and the most highly technical tasks—and per capita income and gross domestic product (GDP) per capita were among the highest in the non-Western world.

Long-range economic development has been directed through a series of five-year plans. The first two five-year plans (1970–75 and 1976–80) established most of the country's basic transport and communications facilities. Subsequent plans sought to diversify the economy; to increase domestic food production; to improve education, vocational training, and health services; and to further improve communications routes between the different regions of the country. But the economic boom was not without a price. As world oil prices stagnated in the 1990s, government policies encouraging larger families led to a marked increase in population. GDP per capita actually began to fall in real terms, and the kingdom's young, highly educated workforce began to face high rates of unemployment and underemployment for the first time. However, those trends reversed as oil prices again rose. In addition, five-year plans were directed toward increasing the share of private enterprise in the economy in an effort to move away from dependence on oil exports and to generate jobs.

AGRICULTURE

At its founding, the kingdom inherited the simple, tribal economy of Arabia. Many of the people were nomads, engaged in raising camels, sheep, and goats. Agricultural production was localized and subsistent. The kingdom's development plans have given domestic food production special attention, and the government has made subsidies and generous incentives available to the agriculture sector. Agriculture now contributes only a small fraction of the Saudi GDP and employs a comparable proportion of the workforce.

Less than 2 percent of the total land area is used for crops. Of the cultivated land, about half consists of rain-fed dry farming (mostly in Asir), two-fifths is in tree crops, and the remainder is irrigated. Most of the irrigated areas—in the districts of Riyadh and Al-Qaṣīm, for example, and near Al-Hufūf in Al-Sharqiyyah province—utilize underground water.

Saudi Arabia has achieved self-sufficiency in the production of wheat, eggs, and milk, among other commodities, though it still imports the bulk of its food needs. Wheat is the primary cultivated grain, followed by sorghum and barley. Dates, melons, tomatoes, potatoes, cucumbers, pumpkins, and squash are also important crops.

Two major constraints on cultivation are poor water supply and poor soil. Concrete and earth-filled dams have been built, primarily in the southwest, to store water for irrigation and as a means of flood control. Agricultural expansion has been great in irrigated areas, while the amount of land given to rain-fed farming has decreased. Substantial resources of subterranean water have been discovered in the central and eastern parts of the country and exploited for agriculture. However, these underground aquifers are difficult to renew.

PETROLEUM

The economy of Saudi Arabia is dominated by petroleum and its associated industries. In terms of oil reserves, Saudi

Arabia ranks first internationally, with about one-fifth of the world's known reserves. Oil deposits are located in the east, southward from Iraq and Kuwait into the Rub' al-Khali and under the waters of the Persian Gulf.

The discovery of oil changed the entire economic situation of Saudi Arabia. As early as 1923, Ibn Sa'ūd granted an oil-prospecting concession to a British company, but this concession was never exploited. Although oil was discovered in 1938, World War II curtailed oil-producing activities until near its end. The Ras Tanura refinery was opened in 1945, and rapid expansion of the oil industry followed to meet increasing postwar demand.

In 1951 the Arabian American Oil Company (Aramco) discovered the first offshore field in the Middle East, at Ra's Al-Saffāniyyah, just south of the former Saudi Arabia–Kuwait neutral zone, and oil was discovered in the zone itself in 1953. Al-Ghawār, just south of Dhahran and west

Flames shoot from an oil refinery vent in Saudi Arabia. The country ranks first globally in oil reserves. W. Robert Moore/National Geographic Image Collection/Getty Images

of Al-Hufūf, is one of the world's largest oil fields. The first portion of the Al-Ghawār oil field was discovered at 'Ayn Dār in 1948. Intensive exploration of the Rub' al-Khali began in 1950, and oil fields were finally discovered in the area in the 1970s.

In 1950 Aramco put into operation the Trans-Arabian Pipe Line (Tapline), which ran from Al-Qayṣūmah in Saudi Arabia across Jordan and Syria to its Mediterranean terminal at Sidon, Leb. The line was in operation only sporadically during the 1970s, and in 1983 it ceased to function beyond supplying a refinery in Jordan. In 1981 Petroline, built to carry crude oil, was completed from Al-Jubayl on the Persian Gulf to Yanbu' on the Red Sea, and this greatly shortened the distance to Europe and obviated navigation through the gulf and the Strait of Hormuz. Petroline was built by the General Petroleum and Mineral Organization (Petromin), a government-owned corporation. Aramco constructed a massive gas-gathering system and, parallel to Petroline, a pipeline for transporting natural-gas liquids, which reached Yanbu' in 1981.

During the 1970s and early '80s, Saudi Arabia gradually acquired complete ownership of Aramco, and in 1984 Aramco had its first Saudi president. In 1988 the company was renamed Saudi Aramco.

Trans-Arabian Pipeline

The Trans-Arabian Pipeline (also called the Tapline) is a crude oil pipeline extending 1,069 miles (1,720 km) from Al-Dammām on the Persian Gulf coast of Saudi Arabia to Sidon, Leb., on the Mediterranean Sea. The pipeline was built by a subsidiary of Aramco and began operations in 1950; it largely ceased functioning in the early 1980s.

The 315-mile (507-km) portion from Al-Dammām to Al-Qayṣūmah in Saudi Arabia gathered the output of several Saudi oil fields, which was then pumped through the remaining 754 miles (1,213 km) of the pipeline across the deserts of northern Saudi Arabia into Jordan and then northwest across southern Syria and Lebanon. It consisted of 30-inch (760-mm) and 31-inch (790-mm) pipe with an initial capacity of 3 million barrels per day and reached its greatest elevation of 2,975 feet (907 m) in Saudi Arabia just east of the Jordan boundary. The Sidon terminus of the pipeline was one mile offshore at the tanker anchorage; ships were loaded by gravity at the rate of up to 39,000 barrels per hour. During the early 1970s the line was sabotaged and operated only intermittently. Late in the decade, because of rising operating costs the pipeline faced increasing competition from sea transport by supertanker. In 1983 it largely ceased to function beyond supplying a refinery in Jordan.

OTHER RESOURCES

Other mineral resources are known to exist, and the government has pursued a policy of exploration and production in order to diversify the economic base. Geologic reconnaissance mapping of the Precambrian shield in the west has revealed deposits of gold, silver, copper, zinc, lead, iron, titanium, pyrite, magnesite, platinum, and cadmium. There are also nonmetallic resources such as limestone, silica, gypsum, and phosphorite.

Scarcity of water is a perennial problem in the country. Saudi Arabia has the largest single desalination program in the world, which meets most domestic and industrial needs. Underwater aquifers provide a limited amount of potable water, and a great deal of energy has been committed to constructing dams for water storage and to developing water-recycling plants.

Saudi Arabia has relied increasingly on electricity, and electrical production has grown rapidly since the 1970s. Originally highly decentralized, electrical production was slowly centralized under state control during the latter half of the 20th century. In 2000 electrical production was consolidated under a single corporation in an effort to develop a comprehensive national grid. Most of the kingdom's generators are powered by natural gas and diesel fuel.

MANUFACTURING

The manufacturing sector has expanded widely since 1976, when the government established the Saudi Basic Industries Corporation (Sabic) in order to diversify the economy. Its initial goal was to expand the manufacturing potential of sectors of the economy related to petroleum. Since then manufactures, many associated with Sabic, have included rolled steel, petrochemicals, fertilizers, pipes, copper wire and cable, truck assembly, refrigeration, plastics, aluminum products, metal products, and cement. Small-scale enterprises have included baking, printing, and furniture manufacturing.

FINANCE

The Saudi Arabian Monetary Agency (SAMA) was established in 1952 as the kingdom's central money and banking authority. It regulates commercial and development banks and other financial institutions. Its functions include issuing, regulating, and stabilizing the value of the national currency, the riyal; acting as banker for the government; and managing foreign reserves and investments. As an Islamic institution, it has a nonprofit status. Under Islamic law, banks cannot charge interest, but

Ministry of Finance building in Riyadh, Saudi Arabia. Diane Rawson/ Photo Researchers

they do charge fees for lending and pay commission on deposits. Money supply and the tempo of business are dominated by government economic activity, though the government has increasingly favoured expansion of the private sector.

A number of commercial banks operate in the country, some of which are joint ventures between Saudi citizens and foreign banks. (Like all enterprises, banks doing business in the country require a Saudi partner.) Others, however, are wholly owned by Saudis. Banking regulations traditionally have not been stringently enforced, and private banks have shown great flexibility and creativity in interpreting Islamic banking regulations. Moreover, in spite of the ubiquity of banks in the country, large numbers of citizens and expatriates continue to rely on money changers, both for their convenience and for the anonymity that they provide.

TRADE

Exports consist almost entirely of petroleum and petroleum products, the vast majority of which is in the form of crude petroleum. Major imports are machinery and transport equipment, base and fabricated metals, foodstuffs and animals, and chemicals and chemical products. The principal trading partners are the United States, Japan, China, and South Korea. The principal sources of imports are the United States, China, Japan, Germany, and South Korea.

SERVICES

The service sector grew dramatically in the second half of the 20th century with the influx of revenue derived from petroleum sales and because of large levels of government spending. Some three-fifths of workers are engaged in service-related occupations, including civil administration, defense, wholesale and retail sales, and hospitality and tourism. These sectors of the economy account for roughly one-fifth of GDP.

The hospitality industry has traditionally been strong only in and around the holy cities of Mecca and Medina, with the annual influx of pilgrims. However, in the 1960s, large numbers of expatriates—some with their dependents—began to arrive in the country, and facilities began to spring up to meet their needs. Only in the late 20th century did the government actively seek to attract tourists to Saudi Arabia with the construction of a number of coastal resorts and a relaxation of visa requirements for entering the country. Tourism not associated with religious observance, however, remains an extremely small part of GDP.

LABOUR AND TAXATION

Saudi Arabia has traditionally relied on large numbers of foreign labourers, who, at the height of their influx, accounted for roughly two-thirds of the labour force. Most of these have been unskilled or semiskilled workers from other parts of the Middle East and from South Asia, while Westerners, particularly Americans, have filled the most highly skilled positions in the country. Workers in Saudi Arabia have few legal rights, and they are not permitted to organize and do not have the right to strike.

Rapid population growth since the late 20th century has increased the number of native Saudis entering the labour force. Beginning in the 1990s, the government responded by encouraging a policy of "Saudi-ization" (in which employers were required to hire fewer migrant workers), but highly educated young Saudis seemed unwilling to engage in occupations that had been traditionally filled by expatriates and were therefore considered menial. Female citizens traditionally have had limited employment opportunities outside the home, with most occupations being restricted to men. Many foreign women have been employed as domestic servants.

Roughly three-fourths of government revenues are derived from the proceeds of oil exports. Remaining revenues are raised through tariffs, licensing fees, and the proceeds of government investments. Foreign companies are required to pay an income tax, but exemptions are often granted. Saudi citizens are required to pay the *zakāt*, an obligatory tax on Muslims that is used to help the less fortunate in society.

Zakāt

The *zakāt* is an obligatory tax required of Muslims and one of the five Pillars of Islam. The *zakāt* is levied on five categories of property—food grains; fruit; camels, cattle, sheep, and goats; gold and silver; and movable goods—and is payable each year after one year's possession. The tax levy required by religious law varies with the category. Recipients of the *zakāt* include the poor and needy, the collectors themselves, and "those whose hearts it is necessary to conciliate"—e.g., discordant tribesmen, debtors, volunteers in jihad (holy war), and pilgrims.

Under the caliphates, the collection and expenditure of *zakāt* was a function of the state. In the contemporary Muslim world it has been left up to the individual, except in such countries as Saudi Arabia, where the Sharīʿah (Islamic law) is strictly maintained. Among the Ithnā ʿAshariyyah (Twelver Shīʿites), it is collected and disbursed by the community of scholars called the ulama (Arabic: *ʿulamāʾ*), who act as representatives for Muḥammad al-Mahdī al-Ḥujjah (the Hidden Imam).

The Qurʾān and Hadith (sayings and actions of the Prophet Muhammad) also stress *ṣadaqah*, or voluntary almsgiving, which, like *zakāt*, is intended for the needy. Twelver Shīʿites, moreover, require payment of an additional one-fifth tax, the *khums*, to the Hidden Imam and his deputies. It is intended to be spent for the benefit of the imams in addition to orphans, the poor, and travelers.

TRANSPORTATION AND TELECOMMUNICATIONS

Saudi Arabia's roads are all paved, and the automobile is a common form of transport. Taxis are found in cities and most large towns. Women are not permitted to drive. The first coast-to-coast road connection, from Al-Dammām on the gulf to Jiddah on the Red Sea, by way of Riyadh,

Terminal building at Dhahran International Airport, Dhahran, Saudi Arabia. The J. Allan Cash Photolibrary

was opened in 1967. It includes a spectacular descent of the western escarpment from Al-Ṭā'if to Mecca. A causeway, opened in 1986, connects the kingdom with the island country of Bahrain. A railroad passing through Al-Hufūf connects Riyadh and Al-Dammām.

Seaport capacity has been greatly expanded. Major cargo ports are Jiddah, Yanbuʿ, Ḍibā, and Jīzān on the Red Sea and Al-Dammām and Al-Jubayl on the gulf. The country has many small airports and airfields. The national airline, Saudi Arabian Airlines (formerly Saudia; founded 1945), provides both domestic and international service. The chief international airports are at Dhahran, Riyadh, and Jiddah.

Radio broadcasts began in the kingdom in 1948, and the first television station was established in 1965. All broadcasts are operated by the state, and programming focuses on religious and cultural affairs, news, and other topics that are viewed as edifying by the government. Radio and television services are widely accessible, as is telephone service. The government has invested significant resources in updating and expanding the country's telecommunications infrastructure, and large portions of the telephone grid have been digitized. Cellular telephone service is widespread, and access to the Internet is available in all major population centres.

CHAPTER 3

Saudi Arabian Government and Society

Saudi Arabia is a monarchy ruled by the Āl Saʿūd, a family whose status was established by its close ties with and support for the Wahhābī religious establishment. Islamic law, the Sharīʿah, is the primary source of legislation, but the actual promulgation of legislation and implementation of policy is often mitigated by more mundane factors, such as political expediency, the inner politics of the ruling family, and the influence of intertribal politics, which remain strong in the modern kingdom.

In the end, however, all major policy decisions are made outside these formal apparatuses. Decisions are made through a consensus of opinion that is sought primarily within the royal family (comprising the numerous descendants of the kingdom's founder, Ibn Saʿūd), many of whom hold sensitive government posts. Likewise, the views of important members of the ulama (religious scholars), leading tribal sheikhs, and heads of prominent commercial families are considered.

LOCAL GOVERNMENT

Saudi Arabia is divided into administrative regions (*manāṭiq*), which in turn are divided into numerous districts. Regional governors are appointed, usually from the royal family, and preside over one or more municipal councils, half of whose members are appointed and half elected. With their councils, the governors are responsible for such functions as finance, health, education, agriculture, and municipalities. The consultative principle operates at all levels of government, including the government of villages and tribes.

Saudi Arabia's King Fahd. It was during Fahd's reign (1982–2005) that the Basic Law of Government was passed. Joseph Barrack/AFP/Getty Images

JUSTICE

The Sharīʿah is the basis of justice. Judgment usually is according to the Ḥanbalī tradition of Islam; the law tends to be conservative and punishment severe, including amputation for crimes such as theft and execution for crimes that are deemed more severe (e.g., drug trafficking and practicing witchcraft).

In 1970 the Ministry of Justice was established; its work is assisted by a Supreme Judicial Council consisting of leading members of the ulama. There are more than 300 Sharīʿah courts across the country. Rapid changes since the mid-20th century have produced circumstances—such as traffic violations and industrial accidents—not encompassed by traditional law, and these have been handled by the issuance of royal decrees. These decrees have evolved into a body of administrative law that is not directly drawn from Islamic precepts. Avenues of appeal are available, and the monarch is both the final court of appeal and the dispenser of pardon.

Ḥanbalī School of Law

The Ḥanbalī legal school is the most fundamentalist of the four Sunni schools of religious law. Based on the teachings of Aḥmad ibn Ḥanbal (780–855), the Ḥanbalī legal school (*madhhab*) emphasized virtually complete dependence on the divine in the establishment of legal theory and rejected personal opinion (*raʾy*), analogy (*qiyās*), and the Hellenistic dogma of the Muʿtazilah school of theology, on the grounds that human speculation is likely to introduce sinful innovations (*bidʿah*). The school thus relied solely on a literal reading of the Qurʾān and Hadith (narratives relating to the Prophet's life and sayings) in formulating legal decisions. Popular in Iraq and Syria until the 14th century, the traditionalist Ḥanbalī legal approach was revived in the 18th century through the teachings of Ibn Taymiyyah (1263–1328) in the Wahhābī movement of central Arabia. This *madhhab* has since become the official legal school of 20th-century Saudi Arabia.

POLITICAL PROCESS

Participation in the political process is limited to a relatively small portion of the population. There are no elections for national bodies, political parties are outlawed, and women have few political rights. Power rests largely in the hands of the royal family, which governs through a process that—in spite of the political and economic changes since the late 20th century—differs little from the traditional system of tribal rule. Tribal identity remains strong and is still an important pillar of social control; in spite of the existence of a modern state bureaucracy, political influence is frequently determined by tribal affiliation. Tribal sheikhs, therefore, maintain a high degree of authority within the tribe and a considerable degree of influence over local and national events.

The tribal hierarchy in the country is complex. There are a number of smaller, less-influential tribes and a handful of very influential major tribes. The Saʿūd family, although not a tribe strictly speaking, behaves like one in many respects. Although the ruling family came to power largely through its martial skill and religious ties, its continued hegemony has been based on the traditional view in Arabian society that leaders owe their positions to their ability to manage affairs. Just as the tribal sheikh leads the tribe, so has the Saʿūd family ruled the country—by placating rival factions, building a broad consensus, and squelching extreme voices. (Early Orientalists used the Latin phrase *primus inter pares*, "first among equals," to refer to such an arrangement.) The medium for this process is the traditional *dīwān*, an informal council in which the senior male (whether he is a sheikh at the tribal level or the king at the national) hears outstanding grievances and dispenses justice and largess. In theory, any male citizen may make his voice heard in the *dīwān*.

In this system, succession to the throne is not directly hereditary, though, under the Basic Law of Government, the king must be a son or grandson of Ibn Saʿūd. Traditionally the heir apparent, who is also deputy prime minister, has been determined by a consensus of the royal family, but since 1992 he has been appointed by the king (confirmation by the family occurring only after the monarch's death). In the same way, through consensus, the family may depose the monarch, as was seen in King Saʿūd's deposition in 1964.

The family has also relied heavily on its long relationship with the Wahhābī religious hierarchy to maintain social and political control. The crown appoints all major religious functionaries, who are almost exclusively selected from Wahhābī ulama; in turn it is supported by that sect. Most major threats to the political status quo have come either from dissident factions within the religious community or from groups that appeal in some way to Islamic values. Many of these groups have operated abroad, and a number have been involved in political violence.

SECURITY

Military service is voluntary. The army accounts for about three-fifths of the total military force. It experienced rapid modernization especially after the June (Six-Day) War of 1967. The air force was equipped largely by the British until the 1970s, when the kingdom began to buy aircraft from the United States. It is now one of the best-equipped forces in the region, with several hundred high-performance aircraft; likewise, ground forces have large numbers of state-of-the-art main battle tanks. Army officers are trained at King ʿAbd al-ʿAzīz Military Academy just north of Riyadh. Major air bases are at Riyadh, Dhahran, Ḥafar al-Bāṭin (part of the King Khālid

Military City) near the border with Iraq and Kuwait, Tabūk in the northwest near Jordan, and Khamīs Mushayṭ in the southwest near Yemen. All three armed services—army, air force, and navy—are directed by the defense minister, who is also the second deputy prime minister.

The National Guard, which has roughly the same troop strength as the army, is essentially an internal security force, though it can support the regular forces for national defense. One of its primary peacetime tasks is to guard the country's oil fields. It is administered separately, and its commander reports to the crown prince. The armed forces employ expatriate personnel in support and training positions.

The kingdom has several internal security organs, including the Coast Guard, Frontier Force, and a centralized national police force. All of these organizations report to the Ministry of the Interior, which also supervises the country's intelligence and counterintelligence bodies. Police interaction with civilians, particularly with foreigners, has often been described as heavy-handed, but reports of human rights abuses are far less numerous and severe than those reported in other countries of the region. There is also a religious police force attached to the Committee for the Promotion of Virtue and the Prevention of Vice. Known as the Muṭawwaʿūn (colloquially, Muṭawwaʿīn), this force operates in plain clothes and enforces such Islamic precepts as ensuring that women are properly veiled, that shops close during prayer, and that the fast is kept during Ramadan. Imposing impromptu corporal punishment for infractions is an accepted part of their duty.

Health and Welfare

A great deal of attention has been given to health care, and the numbers of hospital beds, physicians, and nurses

Essentially an internal security force, the Saudi Arabian National Guard is also charged with protecting the country's oil reserves. Bilal Qabalan/AFP/Getty Images

have increased greatly. In addition to numerous health institutes, hospitals, and health centres, a network of dispensaries serving communities of 10,000 or more people has been set up, complemented by a system of mobile health services reaching small communities and the remaining nomadic populations. The government has also begun to train Saudis to replace foreign medical personnel. Of serious concern are a high rate of trachoma and occasional outbreaks of malaria, schistosomiasis, and cholera. Outbreaks of serious diseases such as meningitis have occurred during the hajj.

HOUSING

Because of the kingdom's geographic diversity, a wide variety of traditional housing types were embraced. These ranged from the conventional black tents of the Bedouin and mud-brick dwellings of agrarian villages to the lofty, ornate townhouses found in urban centres along the coast. Since the advent of oil wealth, the government has invested heavily in housing construction. It provides low-interest or interest-free loans to citizens wishing to purchase or build homes. Homes in newer areas are equipped with standard utilities (such as water, sewerage, and electricity) as well as many technical conveniences, such as Internet access and cable and satellite television. Towns in some rural areas, however, remain far removed from power and water networks.

EDUCATION

Education is free at all levels and is given high priority by the government. The school system consists of elementary (grades 1–6), intermediate (7–9), and secondary (10–12) schools. A significant portion of the curriculum at

Mud dwellings with crenellated rooftops typical of Najrān, Asir region, Saudi Arabia. Peter Ryan/Robert Harding Picture Library

all levels is devoted to religious subjects, and, at the secondary level, students are able to follow either a religious or a technical track. Girls are able to attend school (all courses are segregated by gender), but fewer girls attend than boys. This disproportion is reflected in the rate of literacy, which is about 90 percent among males and is about 80 percent among females.

Higher education has expanded at a remarkable pace. Institutions of higher education include the King Saʿūd University (formerly the University of Riyadh, founded in 1957), the Islamic University (1961) at Medina, and the King Abdulaziz University (1967) in Jiddah. Other colleges and universities emphasize curricula in sciences and technology, military studies, religion, and medicine. Institutes devoted to Islamic studies in particular abound, and schools for religious pedagogy are located in several towns. Women typically receive college instruction in segregated institutions. Many foreign teachers are employed, especially in technical and medical schools. Large numbers of students travel abroad for university study.

In an effort to improve Saudi Arabia's status as a regional scientific hub and to help it compete in the sciences on an international level, in September 2009 the King Abdullah University of Science and Technology was opened near Jiddah. The campus hosted state-of-the-art laboratories, virtual reality facilities, and one of the world's most powerful supercomputers. The coed university—many of whose students were drawn from abroad—strove to provide a comparatively liberal environment relative to the rest of Saudi society. Women were permitted to drive on campus and were free to veil or unveil at their discretion.

CHAPTER 4

Saudi Arabian Cultural Life

The Saudi cultural setting is Arab and Muslim. To preserve the country's purist religious position, many proscriptions of behaviour and dress are enforced. Alcoholic beverages are prohibited, for example, and there is no theatre or public exhibition of films. Educated Saudis are well informed on issues of the Arab world, the Muslim world, and the world at large, but public expression of opinion about domestic matters is not encouraged. There are no organizations such as political parties or labour unions to provide public forums.

DAILY LIFE AND SOCIAL CUSTOMS

Saudi Arabia's population has traditionally been composed of nomads, villagers, and townspeople. Pervading this triad, however, is the patrilineal kinship principle, and superimposed on all is the administrative organization centred on the royal family. The kinship principle is pervasive in Saudi society, and the extended family is a strong social unit. Villages constitute local service centres and contain members from more than one tribal affiliation, though one group may tend to be dominant. Cities are not tribally organized, though the importance of kinship affiliation endures, and local affairs tend to be dominated and administered by a few families.

Social stratification is more clearly developed in the cities than elsewhere. Before the effects of oil were felt on the economy, status was a matter of lineage and occupation rather than of wealth. With the development of the oil industry, however, wealth and material position have acquired an additional social value. The new technology and industry have produced a growing middle-income

Saudi shopkeepers dressed in traditional garb, including the thwab *and* kaffiyeh, *converse along the streets of Jiddah's main bazaar.* Kaveh Kazemi/Hulton Archive/Getty Images

economic group of technocrats that is increasingly aware of the widening gap between the ruling families and the rest of the population. This has led to discontent and, in some cases, outbreaks of civil unrest.

Most Saudis continue to dress in a traditional fashion. For men this consists of an ankle-length shirt known as a *thawb* (or *dishdashah*), which is usually woven of white cotton. The traditional head cover is the kaffiyeh (sometimes known as a *ghuṭrah*), a broad cloth folded and held in place by a camel's hair cord known as an *ʿiqāl*. The time-honoured dress for women consists of a *thawb* beneath which is worn a loose fitting pair of slacks known as a *sirwāl*. In public women are expected to be fully veiled, however, and a long black cloak known as an *ʿabāyah* is worn. A veil called a *ḥijāb* covers the head, and another known as a *niqāb* covers the face. Among Bedouin, women's clothing is often quite ornate and has traditionally consisted of a beautiful panoply of handcrafted silver jewelry.

Cuisine in Saudi Arabia is broadly similar to that of the surrounding Persian Gulf countries, and Turkish, Persian, and African cultures have heavily influenced culinary tastes. Islamic dietary customs are closely observed; for instance, pork is not consumed, wine is eschewed, and even ritually licit animals such as lambs must be slaughtered in a prescribed fashion. A dish consisting of a stuffed lamb, known as *khūzī*, is the traditional national favourite. Kebabs are also popular, as is *shāwarmah* (*shwarma*), a marinated meat dish of lamb, mutton, or chicken that is grilled on a spit and served either as an entrée or a sandwich. As in the countries of the Persian Gulf, *makhbūs* (*machbous*), a rice dish with fish or shrimp, is extremely popular. Flat, unleavened bread is a staple of virtually every meal, as are all varieties of fresh fruit. Dates, either fresh or candied, are ubiquitous. Coffee, served strong and hot in the Turkish style, is the traditional beverage.

In accordance with the Wahhābī interpretation of Islam, only two religious holidays, ʿĪd al-Fiṭr and ʿĪd al-Aḍḥā, are publicly recognized. The celebration of other Islamic holidays, such as the Prophet's birthday and ʿĀshūrāʾ—an important holiday to Shīʿites—are tolerated only when celebrated on a small scale at the local level but are otherwise condemned as dangerous innovations. Public observance of non-Islamic religious holidays is prohibited, with the exception of September 23, which celebrates the unification of the kingdom. (It is also the only holiday celebrated on the Western calendar.)

THE ARTS

For a thousand years, artistic expression usually perpetuated ancient forms. From the 18th century onward, the strict Wahhābī religious outlook discouraged intellectual deviation from accepted purist positions. With the advent of the petroleum industry came exposure to outside influences, such as Western housing styles, furnishings, and clothes, and, at the same time, local craftsmen found themselves in competition with imported goods.

Music and dance have always been part of Saudi life. Native music, of which there are several types, is generally associated with poetry and is sung collectively. Instruments include the *rabābah*, an instrument not unlike a three-string fiddle, and various types of percussion instruments, such as the *ṭabl* (drum) and the *ṭār* (tambourine). Of the native dances, the most popular is a martial line dance known as the *ʿarḍah*, which includes lines of men, frequently armed with swords or rifles, dancing to the beat of drums and tambourines.

Native Bedouin poetry, known as *nabaṭī*, is extremely popular. It has similarities to the classical *qaṣīdah*, or ode, of which the central and eastern regions of the country

Traditional designs adorn the doors and walls of a building in Saudi Arabia. Jodi Cobb/National Geographic Image Collection/Getty Images

are the traditional birthplace. Many of the great masters of pre-Islamic Arabic poetry dwelt in what is now Saudi Arabia, and the two styles, *qaṣīdah* and *nabaṭī*, differ largely in the former's use of Classical Arabic as a medium. *Nabaṭī* poetry is composed in the vernacular and has a strong musical quality.

Visual arts are dominated by geometric, floral, and abstract designs and by calligraphy, the latter a sophisticated and learned enterprise. Not much diversity is seen in traditional architecture; typical features are decorative designs on doors and windows and wide use of crenellated walls. The wave of change starting in the 1960s influenced architectural styles, and stark linear motifs became common in office and residential buildings. The spectacular airport terminals at Jiddah and Riyadh, however, are testimony to the persistence of traditional styles.

Qaṣīdah

The *qaṣīdah* is a poetic form developed in pre-Islamic Arabia and perpetuated throughout Islamic literary history into the present. It is a laudatory, elegiac, or satiric poem that is found in Arabic, Persian, and many related Asian literatures. The classic *qaṣīdah* is an elaborately structured ode of 60 to 100 lines, maintaining a single end rhyme that runs through the entire piece; the same rhyme also occurs at the end of the first hemistich (half-line) of the first verse. Virtually any metre is acceptable for the *qaṣīdah* except the *rajaz*, which has lines only half the length of those in other metres.

The *qaṣīdah* opens with a short prelude, the *nasīb*, which is elegiac in mood and is intended to gain the audience's involvement. The *nasīb* depicts the poet stopping at an old tribal encampment to reminisce about the happiness he shared there with his beloved and about his sorrow when they parted; Imru' al-Qays is said to have been the first to use this device, and nearly all subsequent authors of *qaṣīdah* imitate him. After this conventional beginning follows the *raḥīl*, which consists of descriptions of the poet's horse or camel or of desert animals and scenes of desert events and Bedouin life and warfare; it may conclude with a piece on *fakhr*, or self-praise. The main theme, the *madīḥ*, or panegyric, often coupled with *hijā'* (satire of enemies), is last and is the poet's tribute to himself, his tribe, or his patron.

The *qaṣīdah* has always been respected as the highest form of the poetic art and as the special forte of the pre-Islamic poets. While poets with a classical tendency maintained the genre, with its confining rules, the changed circumstances of the Arabs made it an artificial convention. Thus, by the end of the 8th century the *qaṣīdah* had begun to decline in popularity. It was successfully restored for a brief period in the 10th century by al-Mutanabbī and has continued to be cultivated by the Bedouin. *Qaṣīdahs* were also written in Persian, Turkish, and Urdu until the 19th century.

CULTURAL INSTITUTIONS

The King Fahd National Library (founded 1968) is located in Riyadh, as is the National Museum (1978). There are a number of smaller libraries and museums throughout the country, mostly in the larger towns and cities. The Society for Arts and Cultures was founded in 1972 to coordinate and support traditional Arabian art forms. The King Fayṣal Foundation (1976) supports literary, educational, and cultural programs. The annual Jinādiriyyah Heritage and Cultural Festival brings together thousands near Riyadh to partake in traditional pastimes such as camel racing, arts and crafts, and traditional song and dance. Al-Ḥijr (Madāʾin Ṣāliḥ), an archaeological site inhabited until the 1st century CE by the Nabataeans, was designated a UNESCO World Heritage site in 2008.

SPORTS AND RECREATION

Saudis value a number of traditional and modern pastimes. Football (soccer) is extremely popular. Many Saudis also participate in activities such as scuba diving, windsurfing, and sailing. The time-honoured pursuit of camel racing developed a new following in the 1970s, and during the winter—the coolest part of the year—races are held weekly at the Riyadh stadium. The annual King's Camel Race, begun in 1974, is one of the sport's most important contests and attracts animals and riders from throughout the region. Falconry, another traditional pursuit, is still practiced, although it has come under increasingly strict regulation because several species on which the falcon preys have become endangered.

The government of Saudi Arabia has encouraged sports and athletics by constructing sports and recreation facilities in all major urban areas. The Saudi Arabian Olympic Committee was organized in 1964 and was recognized internationally the following year. It has sent athletes to

The annual King's Camel Race in Riyadh, Saudi Arabia. Although this particular contest started in 1974, the tradition of racing camels dates back for centuries. Jodi Cobb/National Geographic Image Collection/Getty Images

the Summer Games since 1972 but has not fielded a team for the Winter Games. The country also sends athletes to the Asian Games.

MEDIA AND PUBLISHING

Several daily and weekly newspapers are published in Arabic and in English. Although newspapers and periodicals are mostly privately owned, editors frequently practice self-censorship. Criticism of the government and of the royal family is frowned upon, and on occasion journalists have been dismissed for statements seen as antigovernment or against religion. The government heavily subsidizes the publishing industry, including periodical and academic presses. Radio and television broadcasting is operated by the Ministry of Information.

CHAPTER 5

Saudi Arabia: Past and Present

The coastal parts of the territory that was to become Saudi Arabia participated in the broad trends of Arabian Peninsula history in the Islamic period—the rise of Islam in western Arabia in the 7th century, the creation and expansion of the various Islamic empires to the 10th century, the establishment of separate and usually small Muslim states in the period leading to the 15th century, and the ordering of the Arab Middle East conducted by the Ottoman Empire starting in the 16th century. Central Arabia was linked commercially and intellectually with western Arabia and the Fertile Crescent but was often isolated from general political and military trends because of its remoteness and relative poverty. In the middle of the 18th century in central Arabia, an alliance of Muslim Wahhābī religious reformers and the Saʿūdī dynasty formed a new state and society that resulted in the creation of three successive Saʿūdī kingdoms, including the modern country of Saudi Arabia, officially proclaimed in 1932.

The Wahhābī Movement

As the population of the oasis towns of central Arabia such as ʿUyaynah slowly grew from the 16th to the early 18th century, the ulama residing there increased in number and sophistication. Muḥammad ibn ʿAbd al-Wahhāb, the founder of the Wahhābī movement, was born in ʿUyaynah in 1703 to a family of religious judges and scholars and as a young man traveled widely in other regions of the Middle East. It was upon his return to ʿUyaynah that he first began to preach his revolutionary ideas of conservative religious reformation based on a strict moral code.

His teaching was influenced by that of the 14th-century Ḥanbalī scholar Ibn Taymiyyah, who called for the purification of Islam through the expulsion of practices that he saw as innovations, including speculative theology, Sufism, and such popular religious practices as saint worship.

The ruler of ʿUyaynah, ʿUthmān ibn Muʿammar, gladly welcomed the returning prodigal and even adhered to his doctrines. But many opposed him, and ʿAbd al-Wahhāb's preaching was put to a number of severe tests. The chief of the Al-Hasa region, who was of the influential Banū Khālid tribe, threatened to withhold gifts to ʿUthmān, or even to go to war with him, unless ʿAbd al-Wahhāb was put to death.

ʿUthmān, unable to face this danger but unwilling to kill his guest, decided to dismiss ʿAbd al-Wahhāb from his territory. ʿAbd al-Wahhāb went to Al-Dirʿiyyah, some 40 miles (65 km) away, which had been the seat of the local prince Muḥammad ibn Saʿūd since 1726. In 1745 people flocked to the teaching of the reformer. The alliance of theologian and prince, duly sealed by mutual oaths of loyalty, soon began to prosper in terms of military success and expansion.

One by one, the enemies of the new union were conquered. The earliest wars brought ʿUyaynah and portions of Al-Hasa under Wahhābī control, but the oasis town of Riyadh maintained a stubborn resistance for 27 years before succumbing to the steady pressure of the new movement. By 1765, when Muḥammad ibn Saʿūd died, only a few parts of central and eastern Arabia had fallen under more or less effective Wahhābī rule.

Muḥammad ibn Saʿūd's son and successor, ʿAbd al-ʿAzīz I (ruled 1765–1803), who had been largely responsible for this extension of his father's realm through his exploits as commander in chief of the Wahhābī forces, continued to work in complete harmony with Muḥammad ibn ʿAbd al-Wahhāb. It was the latter who virtually controlled the civil administration of the country, while ʿAbd al-ʿAzīz himself, later in cooperation with his warlike son, Saʿūd I (ruled 1803–14), busied himself with the expansion of his empire far beyond the limits inherited by him. Meanwhile, in 1792, Muḥammad ibn ʿAbd al-Wahhāb died at the age of 89. Wahhābī attacks on settled areas had begun to attract the attention of officials of the Ottoman Empire, the dominant political force in the region. In 1798 an Ottoman force invaded Al-Hasa, though it later was compelled to withdraw. Qatar fell to the Saʿūdīs in 1797, and they also gained control through local allies over Bahrain and parts of Oman.

In 1801 the Wahhābīs captured and sacked the Shīʿite holy city of Karbalaʾ in Ottoman Iraq, plundering and damaging important religious buildings. In the following year, Saʿūd led his father's army to the capture of Mecca itself in the Hejaz, which was also under Ottoman control. It was soon after Saʿūd's return from this expedition that his father was assassinated by a Shīʿite in the mosque of Al-Dirʿiyyah in revenge for the desecration of Karbalāʾ.

Conflict between the Ottomans and the Wahhābīs of Arabia now broke out in earnest. In 1804 Saʿūd captured Medina, and the Wahhābī empire embraced the whole of Arabia down to Yemen and Oman. Year after year, Saʿūd visited Mecca to preside over the hajj as the imam of the Muslim congregation. But the tide was soon to turn to his disadvantage. The sultan of the Ottoman Empire, preoccupied in other directions, consigned to Muḥammad ʿAlī, the virtually independent viceroy of Egypt, the task of crushing those the Ottomans viewed as heretics. An Egyptian force landed on the Hejaz coast under the command of Muḥammad ʿAlī's son Ṭūsūn. Saʿūd inflicted a severe defeat on the invaders, but reinforcements enabled Ṭūsūn to occupy Mecca and Medina in 1812. The following year, Muḥammad ʿAlī assumed command of the expeditionary force in person. In the east, Britain severely curbed the maritime activities of the Qawāsim dynasty, who were allies of the Wahhābīs, in 1809.

Saʿūd died at Al-Dirʿiyyah in 1814. His successor, his son ʿAbd Allāh ibn Saʿūd, was scarcely of his father's calibre, and the capture of Al-Raʿs in Al-Qaṣīm region by the Egyptians in 1815 forced him to sue for peace. This was duly arranged, but the truce was short-lived, and in 1816 the struggle was renewed, with Ibrāhīm Pasha, another of Muḥammad ʿAlī's sons, in command of the Egyptian forces. Gaining the support of the volatile tribes by skillful diplomacy and lavish gifts, he advanced into central Arabia. Joined by most of the principal tribes, he appeared before Al-Dirʿiyyah in April 1818. Fighting ended in September with the surrender of ʿAbd Allāh, who was sent to the Ottoman capital of Constantinople (Istanbul) and beheaded. Local Wahhābī leaders also were executed, Al-Dirʿiyyah was razed, and Egyptian garrisons were posted to the principal towns.

The Saʿūd family had suffered heavy losses during the fighting. A few had managed to escape before the surrender, yet the rest were sent to Egypt for detention along with descendants of Muḥammad ibn ʿAbd al-Wahhāb. The Wahhābī empire ceased to exist, but the faith lived on in the desert and in the towns of central Arabia in defiance of the new rulers of the land.

SECOND SAʿŪDĪ STATE

The dynasty was restored and the second Saʿūdī state begun in 1824 when Turkī (1823–34), a grandson of Muḥammad ibn Saʿūd, succeeded in capturing Riyadh and expelling the Egyptian garrison. Thereafter, Riyadh remained the capital of the state. Turkī tried to maintain friendly ties with the Ottoman governors of Iraq, as he accepted nominal Ottoman sovereignty, and with the British. Al-Hasa and Ḥā'il fell again to the Sa'ūdīs by 1830 as the town militias of central Arabia, which formed the bases of the Sa'ūdī army, overcame the nomadic tribes. Literature, commerce, and agriculture flourished in spite of the crushing losses to society occasioned by the return of cholera.

In 1834 Turkī was murdered by an ambitious cousin, who then was deposed and executed by Turkī's son Fayṣal (1834–38; 1843–65). Fayṣal had been carried away into captivity in Egypt in 1818 but had escaped in 1828 to rejoin his father and play a prominent part in reestablishing Wahhābī rule. He refused to pay the Egyptian tribute, and in 1837 an Egyptian expeditionary force entered Riyadh. Fayṣal was captured the following year and returned to Cairo. Khālid, son of Sa'ūd and brother of 'Abd Allāh, was installed as ruler of Najd by the Egyptians on the condition that he recognize Egyptian hegemony.

The subservience of Khālid to his Egyptian and Ottoman masters was increasingly resented by his Wahhābī subjects, and in 1841 his cousin, 'Abd Allāh ibn Thunayān, raised the standard of revolt. Riyadh was captured by a bold coup and its garrison was expelled. Khālid, who was in Al-Hasa at the time, fled by ship to Jiddah. 'Abd Allāh resisted when Fayṣal reappeared in 1843, only to be overpowered and slain. So Fayṣal resumed his reign after an interruption of five years and ruled basically unchallenged, in spite of occasional tribal uprisings and friction with the townspeople of Al-Qaṣīm, until his death in 1865. The Hejaz remained in Ottoman hands, while northern Arabia (the province of Jabal Shammar) was locally autonomous but acknowledged the supremacy of Riyadh. Fayṣal reestablished Sa'ūdī authority for a short time in Bahrain and for a longer time in Al-Buraymī and the Oman hinterland. He extended his influence as far as Ḥaḍramawt and the frontiers of Yemen. Only British intervention stopped the extension of direct Saʿūdī power over the western shore of the gulf.

Administration under Fayṣal was simple and involved few people, mostly members of the royal family and descendants of Muḥammad ibn ʿAbd al-Wahhāb. Justice in the provinces was enforced by officials appointed by Riyadh; even the tribes paid taxes. Additionally, the writing of poetry and history flourished.

Death of Fayṣal

In 1865, when his power was an acknowledged factor in Arabian politics, Fayṣal died. His sons disputed the succession. His eldest son, ʿAbd Allāh, succeeded first, maintaining himself against the rebellion of his brother Saʿūd II for six years until the Battle of Jūdah (1871), in which Saʿūd triumphed. ʿAbd Allāh fled, and Saʿūd took power. But during the next five years the throne changed hands no fewer than seven times in favour of different members of the Saʿūd family. Drought in 1870–74 exacerbated the civil war's effects as the unity of the Wahhābī community disintegrated. Meanwhile, ʿAbd Allāh had appealed to the Ottoman governor in Baghdad, who came to his assistance but took advantage of the situation to occupy the province of Al-Hasa for the empire in 1871—an occupation that lasted 42 years.

The Rashīdīs

Saʿūd II died in 1875, and, after a brief interval of chaos, ʿAbd Allāh (as ʿAbd Allāh II) returned to the throne the following year only to find himself powerless against the Rashīdī emirs of Jabal Shammar, with their capital at Ḥā'il. The Rashīdīs had ruled there since 1836, first as agents for the Sa'ūd family, but subsequently they became independent, with strong links to the Ottomans and growing wealth from the caravan trade.

Muḥammad ibn 'Abd Allāh al-Rashīd (ruled 1869–97) was undoubtedly the dominant figure in Arabian politics when 'Abd Allāh (now as 'Abd Allāh II ibn Sa'ūd) returned to Riyadh for his third spell of authority. At first the Rashīdīs refrained from any forward action, but they soon intervened in the chaotic affairs of the Wahhābī state. And it was not long before 'Abd Allāh was persuaded to join Ibn Rashīd at Ḥā'il (ostensibly as a guest but in truth as a hostage), while a representative of the Rashīdīs was appointed governor of Riyadh in 1887. 'Abd Allāh eventually was allowed to return to Riyadh and even was named governor of the city in 1889. 'Abd Allāh did not live to enjoy his restoration for long, however. He died in the same year, leaving to his youngest brother, 'Abd al-Raḥmān, the almost hopeless task of reviving the dynasty.

'Abd al-Raḥmān was soon embroiled in hostilities with the Rashīdīs. The Battle of Al-Mulaydah (in Al-Qaṣīm) settled the issue between them decisively in 1891, and, for the second time in a space of 70 years, the Wahhābī state seemed to be completely destroyed. 'Abd al-Raḥmān fled with his family to take refuge in Kuwait as the guest of its rulers. Unlike the first Sa'ūdī regime, which was ended by external conquest, the second Sa'ūdī state fell chiefly because of internal disputes between members of the royal family.

IBN SA'ŪD AND THE THIRD SA'ŪDĪ STATE

'Abd al-'Azīz (known commonly as Ibn Sa'ūd), the son of the exiled 'Abd al-Raḥmān, took advantage of his new location to acquire useful knowledge of world affairs, while the new Rashīdī prince, ʿAbd al-ʿAzīz ibn ʿAbd Mitʿab, alienated the population of Najd. In 1901 the young Ibn Saʿūd (he was about 22 to 26 years old) sallied out of Kuwait with a force of 40 followers on what must have seemed a forlorn adventure. On Jan. 15, 1902, with a select body of only 15 warriors, he scaled thc walls of Riyadh, surprised and defeated the Rashīdī governor and his escort before the gate of the fort of Mismāk (Musmāk), and was hailed by the populace as their ruler.

The following years witnessed the development of the struggle by the third Saʿūdī state to expand its control once again over most of the Arabian Peninsula and thereby reestablish the glories of the first Saʿūdī state in the 18th century. The first challenge was from the Rashīdīs, whose power was by no means spent and who received substantial help from the Ottomans in men and material. In 1904 Ibn Saʿūd defeated a combined Rashīdī and Ottoman force but afterward allowed the Ottomans to place garrisons in central Arabia for one year. Ibn Rashīd continued the struggle, but he was killed in battle in 1906, and thenceforth Ibn Saʿūd, who secured the withdrawal of Ottoman troops from Al-Qaṣīm in 1906, became the undisputed master of central Arabia. Ibn Saʿūd bent himself to the task of regaining the whole realm of his ancestors. He was cautious enough to continue acknowledging Ottoman overlordship (even if only in name), and, by cultivating contacts with Britain, he hoped to balance each power against the other.

Meanwhile, he busied himself with the reorganization of the country's administration, including the inception of a plan designed to ensure the stability and permanence of his military force. In 1912 he established the first Ikhwān ("Brethren") colony on the desert wells of Al-Arṭāwiyyah, peopled entirely by Bedouin. The colony formed a militant cantonment dedicated to the service of God and prince. During the next decade, nearly 100 similar colonies organized around tribal group identity were founded throughout the country, providing Ibn Saʿūd with a formidable military force. At the same time, however, the Saʿūdī military also included soldiers recruited from the towns and settled areas.

Ibn Saʿūd's first major conquest in Najd was the taking of Al-Hasa province from the Ottomans in 1913, although he was again compelled to reaffirm Ottoman sovereignty over all of his territory in 1914. During World War I (1914–18), he was aided by British subsidies, but he managed by adroit diplomacy to be relatively quiescent, though surrounded by enemies. In 1919, however, he struck his first blow, against Ḥusayn ibn ʿAlī of the Hejaz, whose army was annihilated by the Ikhwān. In 1920 Ibn Saʿūd's son Fayṣal captured the province of Asir between the Hejaz and Yemen. In 1921 Ibn Saʿūd defeated the forces of Muḥammad ibn Ṭalāl, the last Rashīdī emir, and annexed the whole of northern Arabia, occupying Al-Jawf and Wadi Al-Sirḥān in the following year. Kuwait experienced border raids and a Saʿūdī blockade over payment of customs duties. Meanwhile, Fayṣal I and ʿAbdullāh I, the sons of Ḥusayn ibn ʿAlī, had been placed on the thrones of Iraq and Transjordan, respectively, by the British government. These territories and the Hejaz served as a formidable British-protected cordon around the northern and western borders of the Wahhābī state, though incidents along the border were frequent.

In 1923 the British government invited all the rulers concerned in these sporadic hostilities to attend a conference in Kuwait and if possible to settle their differences. The British also made it clear that the subsidies theretofore paid to Ibn Saʿūd and Ḥusayn ibn ʿAlī would be terminated.

The conference ended in complete disagreement, and in September 1924 the Wahhābīs attacked the Hejaz. They captured Al-Ṭā'if after a brief struggle, but this was followed by a massacre of the city's male civilians. The Sa'ūdīs occupied Mecca without opposition. Ibn Sa'ūd then laid siege to Jiddah and Medina, while Ḥusayn ibn 'Alī abdicated his throne in favour of his son 'Alī. By the end of 1925, both Medina and Jiddah had surrendered to the Sa'ūdīs. The Al-'Aqabah–Ma'ān district adjacent to the northern Hejaz was occupied by Transjordan to prevent its falling into Wahhābī hands. On Jan. 8, 1926, Ibn Sa'ūd, who had adopted the title sultan of Najd in 1921, was proclaimed king of the Hejaz in the Great Mosque of Mecca. In 1927 he also changed his title of sultan to king of Najd and its dependencies, the two parts of his dual kingdom being administered for the time being as separate units. In the same year, the Treaty of Jiddah, negotiated between Ibn Sa'ūd and a British special envoy, Sir Gilbert Clayton, placed Sa'ūdī relations with Great Britain on a permanent footing as the British fully acknowledged Sa'ūdī independence. A series of Muslim conferences sponsored by the Sa'ūdīs in the Hejaz legitimized their presence as rulers.

Associating with Christian powers put Ibn Sa'ūd in an awkward position with the more religious elements in Najd. Moreover, his alleged complaisance over British involvement in and protection of Iraq and Transjordan, both of which the Ikhwān thought ripe for conquest, created tension with his military supporters. Incidents on their frontiers created a state of virtual though undeclared war, in which British aircraft played a part in discouraging Wahhābī incursions. Ibn Sa'ūd also on several occasions violently suppressed political and military opposition by the Ikhwān.

Military might and diplomacy, particularly in regard to relations with the British, helped Ibn Saʿūd regain control over much of the Arabian peninsula. General Photographic Agency/Hulton Archive/Getty Images

In 1928 and 1929, Fayṣal al-Dawīsh, Sulṭān ibn Bijād, and other leaders of the Ikhwān, accusing Ibn Saʿūd of betraying the cause for which they had fought and opposing the taxes levied upon their followers, resumed their defiance of the king's authority. The rebels sought to stop the centralization of power in the hands of the king and keep the purity of Wahhābī practices against what they saw as innovations advocated by Ibn Saʿūd. The majority of the population rallied to the king's side, and this, with the support of the Najdi ulama, enabled him to defeat the rebels. The civil war, however, dragged on into 1930, when the rebels were rounded up by the British in Kuwaiti territory and their leaders handed over to the king. With their defeat, power passed definitively into the hands of townspeople rather than the tribes.

Ibn Saʿūd was at last free to give his undivided attention to the development of his country and to the problems of foreign policy that beset him on all sides. Above all, he was concerned to assert and maintain the complete independence of his country and in it the exclusive supremacy of Islam. As long as these fundamental objectives remained in place, he was not only ready to cooperate with all nations but prepared to regard with sympathy some of the practices that had taken root in the Hejaz and other areas as the result of foreign contacts. The ban on music, for example, was progressively circumvented by the radio, which was also used as a tool to unite the kingdom and increase military efficiency. And so the latitudinarian spirit, slowly at first but with ever-increasing momentum, lessened a few of the inhibitions of the puritan regime.

On the other hand, Ibn Saʿūd rigorously opposed the intervention of any foreign government whatever in the internal politics of the regime. Yet, aside from members of the royal family, and Najdi and Hejazi merchants, many of the king's chief advisers were foreign Muslims.

Some of the foreign advisers were political refugees from their homelands and served Ibn Saʿūd for many years.

THE KINGDOM OF SAUDI ARABIA

The history of the Kingdom of Saudi Arabia begins properly on Sept. 23, 1932, when by royal decree the dual kingdom of the Hejaz and Najd with its dependencies, administered since 1927 as two separate units, was unified under the name of the Kingdom of Saudi Arabia. The chief immediate effect was to increase the unity of the kingdom and to decrease the possibility of Hejazi separatism, while the name underscored the central role of the royal family in the kingdom's creation. No attempt was made to change the supreme authority of the king as the absolute monarch of the new regime; indeed, his power was emphasized in 1933 by his choice of his son Saʿūd as heir apparent.

Foreign Relations, 1932–53

From the date of its establishment in September 1932, Saudi Arabia enjoyed full international recognition as an independent state, although it did not join the League of Nations.

In 1934 Ibn Saʿūd was involved in war with Yemen over a boundary dispute. An additional cause of the war was Yemen's support of an uprising by an Asiri prince against Ibn Saʿūd. In a seven-week campaign, the Saudis were generally victorious. Hostilities were terminated by the Treaty of Al-Ṭāʾif, by which the Saudis gained the disputed district. Diplomatic relations with Egypt, severed in 1926 because of an incident on the Meccan pilgrimage, were not renewed until after the death of King Fuʾād of Egypt in 1936.

Fixing the boundaries of the country remained a problem throughout the 1930s. In tribal society, sovereignty was traditionally expressed in the form of suzerainty over certain tribes rather than in fixed territorial boundaries. Hence, Ibn Saʿūd regarded the demarcation of land frontiers with suspicion. Nevertheless, the majority of the frontiers with Iraq, Kuwait, and Jordan had been demarcated by 1930. In the south, no agreement was reached on the exact site of the frontiers with the Trucial States and with the interior of Yemen and Muscat and Oman.

After Saudi Arabia declared its neutrality during World War II (1939–45), Britain and the United States subsidized Saudi Arabia, which declared war on Germany in 1945, and this thus enabled the kingdom to enter the United Nations as a founding member. Ibn Saʿūd also joined the Arab League, but he did not play a leading part in it, since the religious and conservative element in Saudi Arabia opposed cooperation with other Arab states, even when Saudis shared common views, as in opposition to Zionism. In the Arab-Israeli War of 1948, Saudi Arabia contributed only one battalion.

Internal Affairs, 1932–53

Although oil had been discovered in Al-Hasa near the shores of the Persian Gulf before World War II, it was not exploited until after 1941. State revenues before the war were derived primarily from the pilgrimage, customs duties, and taxes—which decreased as a result of the world economic depression of the 1930s. After 1944 large numbers of foreign oil workers arrived in the country, and Aramco (Arabian American Oil Company) was established as a joint venture between a number of American oil companies and the Saudi government. The country was itself unable to supply the oil company with sufficient skilled workers, and oil production was largely managed and undertaken by foreigners. When in 1949 Aramco paid more taxes to the U.S. government than the yield to Saudi

Arabia in royalties, the Saudi leadership obtained a new agreement in 1950 that required Aramco to pay an income tax of 50 percent of the net operating income to the Saudis.

The sudden wealth from increased production was a mixed blessing. Cultural life flourished, primarily in the Hejaz, which was the centre for newspapers and radio, but the large influx of outsiders apparently increased xenophobia in a population already noted for its distrust of foreigners. The disturbance of traditional patterns caused by the cultural changes, new wealth from increased production of oil, inflation, and the movement of the population to the major cities was reflected in the government, which had become increasingly wasteful and lavish. In spite of the new wealth, extravagant spending led to governmental deficits and foreign borrowing in the 1950s.

Ibn Saʿūd, who had been brought up in the strict puritanical faith of the Wahhābīs, viewed this flood of wealth and the consequent changing mores with distaste and bewilderment. He died on Nov. 9, 1953.

Saudi Aramco

Saudi Aramco, established in 1933 as Aramco (Arabian American Oil Company), is an oil company founded by the Standard Oil Co. of California (Chevron) when the government of Saudi Arabia granted it a concession. Other U.S. companies joined after oil was found near Dhahran in 1938. In 1950 Aramco opened a pipeline from Saudi Arabia to the Mediterranean Sea port of Sidon, Leb. It was closed in 1983 except to supply a refinery in Jordan. A more successful pipeline, with a destination on the Persian Gulf, was finished in 1981. In 1951 Aramco found the first offshore oil field in the Middle East. In the 1970s and '80s, control gradually passed to the Saudi Arabian government, which eventually took over Aramco and renamed it Saudi Aramco in 1988.

Reigns of Sa'ud ibn 'Abd al-'Aziz and Fayṣal (1953–75)

Ibn Sa'ūd was succeeded by his eldest surviving son, Sa'ūd, with his second son, Fayṣal (Sa'ūd's half brother), declared heir apparent. The two half-brothers were remarkably different. Sa'ūd had been heir apparent since 1933; he had many ties among the desert tribes. Fayṣal, who had lived chiefly in the cities of the Hejaz, had often been abroad in his post as Saudi foreign minister. Sa'ūd thus represented what soon would become the ancien régime, while those advocating modernization supported Fayṣal.

Meanwhile, money continued to pour into the country. There was an enormous increase in the population of the towns, notably of Riyadh and Jiddah. The character of these urban societies was changed beyond all recognition by a large influx of bourgeoisie from neighbouring countries. The freer lifestyle of immigrant wives was tolerated to a certain degree, but such liberalization was not extended to Saudi women. Roads, schools, hospitals, palaces, apartment buildings, and airports replaced the old alleyways and mud-brick houses. Weaving and other crafts continued, but they were modified by the use of new patterns and materials.

At the royal court, there was constant rivalry between Sa'ūd and Fayṣal. In March 1958, as a result of pressure from the royal family, Sa'ūd issued a decree transferring all executive power to Fayṣal. In December 1960, however, Fayṣal was obliged to resign as prime minister, and the king himself assumed the office. In 1962–63 Fayṣal was once more given executive powers. Finally, on Nov. 2, 1964, the family collectively deposed Sa'ūd and proclaimed Fayṣal king. The National Guard, the royal princes, and the ulama had supported Fayṣal in the struggle for power against Sa'ūd. Fayṣal was simply more competent than Sa'ūd. It was he who developed the ministries of government and established for the first time an efficient bureaucracy.

Since the frontier between Saudi Arabia and Oman had never been demarcated and because there was the possibility of discovering oil in the area, in 1952 Saudi Arabian forces occupied the oasis of Al-Buraymī, which Britain felt belonged to Oman and the emirate of Abu Dhabi (Abū Ẓaby)—both of which enjoyed British protection. In July 1954 the British and Saudi governments agreed to submit the dispute to an arbitration tribunal. The tribunal convened in Geneva in September 1955, but the negotiations broke down, and British-officered forces from Oman and Abu Dhabi reoccupied the oasis. During the Suez Crisis in 1956, Saudi Arabia broke off relations with Britain, and they were not reestablished until 1963. In September 1961, following the Iraqi claim to sovereignty over Kuwait, Saudi Arabia sent troops to Kuwait in response to a request from its ruler.

Since World War II, the United States had become the most influential foreign power in Saudi Arabia. American interest was directed toward the oil industry, which was owned by U.S. companies. In 1960 Saudi Arabia helped found the Organization of the Petroleum Exporting Countries (OPEC). The Saudis favoured the United States in the Cold War with the Soviet Union, but they opposed American support of Israel.

As a result of the rise to power of Egypt's Pan-Arab nationalist president Gamal Abdel Nasser, Saudi relations with Egypt were often strained. Egyptian propaganda made frequent attacks on the Saudi system of royal government. When Egyptian troops were sent to North Yemen in 1962, tension between Saudi Arabia and Egypt became more acute. The Saudis helped the Yemeni royalists against the Egyptian-backed Yemen republic. King

Fayṣal ultimately agreed to assist Egypt with financial aid, provided Nasser withdrew his troops from Yemen.

Fayṣal, leader of the largest conservative Arab state, continued to warn against the danger of communist influence in Arab and Muslim countries. Saudi Arabia also acted against the United States, however, as a result of U.S. assistance to Israel during the October (Yom Kippur) War of 1973. The Saudis and other Arab oil producers organized a short-lived oil boycott, and the price of oil worldwide quadrupled.

The Saudi government gained direct ownership of one-fourth of Aramco's crude oil operations in 1973. Ultimately, the Saudis achieved complete control of the company and, therefore, over their chief economic resource. By 1984 the president of Aramco was a Saudi citizen.

OPEC

OPEC (known in full as the Organization of the Petroleum Exporting Countries) is a multinational organization that was established to coordinate the petroleum policies of its members and to provide member states with technical and economic aid. OPEC was established in September 1960 and formally constituted in January 1961 by five countries: Saudi Arabia, Iran, Iraq, Kuwait, and Venezuela. Members admitted afterward include Qatar (1961), Indonesia and Libya (1962), Abu Dhabi (1967), Algeria (1969), and Nigeria (1971). The United Arab Emirates—which includes Abu Dhabi (the largest of the emirates), Dubai, ʿAjmān, Al-Shāriqah, Umm al-Qaywayn, Ra's al-Khaymah, and Al-Fujayrah—assumed Abu Dhabi membership in the 1970s. Ecuador withdrew from OPEC in December 1992, followed by Gabon in January 1995; neither country, however, held large oil reserves or was a large oil producer. In 2007 Angola officially joined OPEC.

OPEC members collectively own about two-thirds of the world's proven petroleum reserves and account for two-fifths of world oil production. Members differ in a variety of ways, including the size of oil reserves, geography, religion, and economic and political interests. Four members—Kuwait, Qatar, Saudi Arabia, and the United Arab Emirates—have very large per capita oil reserves. They also are relatively strong financially and thus have considerable flexibility in adjusting their production. Saudi Arabia, which has the largest reserves and a relatively small (but fast-growing) population, has traditionally played a dominant role in determining overall production and prices.

The influence of individual OPEC members on the organization and on the oil market usually depends on their levels of reserves and production. Saudi Arabia, which controls about one-third of OPEC's total oil reserves, plays a leading role in the organization. Other important members are Iran, Iraq, Kuwait, and the United Arab Emirates, whose combined reserves are significantly greater than those of Saudi Arabia. Kuwait, which has a very small population, has shown a willingness to cut production relative to the size of its reserves, whereas Iran and Iraq, both with large and growing populations, have generally produced at high levels relative to reserves. Revolutions and wars have impaired the ability of some OPEC members to maintain high levels of production.

Reign of Khālid (1975–82)

On March 25, 1975, King Fayṣal was assassinated. He was succeeded by his half-brother, Crown Prince Khālid, and Prince Fahd was made crown prince. During the new king's reign, economic and social development continued at an extremely rapid rate, revolutionizing the infrastructure and educational system of the country.

After the signing of the Egyptian-Israeli peace agreement on March 26, 1979, Saudi Arabia joined most of the other Arab nations in severing diplomatic relations with Egypt. The establishment of the Islamic Republic of Iran

Pilgrims being held hostage during a November 1979 raid on the Great Mosque in Mecca, staged by militants angered by perceived shortcomings of the Saudi royal family. AFP/Getty Images

in 1979 and the subsequent Iran-Iraq War (1980–88) also caused the Saudi monarchy serious concern—owing in no small part to the large Shīʿite minority in eastern Saudi Arabia (the same sect that predominates in Iran) that rioted in 1979 and 1980 in support of Iran's revolution. The kingdom thereafter supported Iraq in its war with Iran.

A dramatic domestic challenge to the monarchy took place in November 1979 when the Ḥaram mosque (Great Mosque) in Mecca, the holiest site in the world for Muslims, was seized by followers of a Saudi religious extremist, Juhaymān al-ʿUtaybī, who had been educated by the Saudi religious establishment and was a former member of the National Guard. Juhaymān protested what he saw as the un-Islamic behaviour of the Saudi royal family. The rebels occupied the mosque for two weeks before they were defeated by National Guard troops.

Saudi Arabia under Fahd and Crown Prince ʿAbd Allāh (1982–2005)

On June 13, 1982, King Khālid died, and Crown Prince Fahd, who had long been influential in the administration of affairs, acceded to the throne. Fahd maintained Saudi Arabia's foreign policy of close cooperation with the United States and increased purchases of sophisticated military equipment from the United States and Britain. In the 1970s and '80s, Saudi Arabia had become the single largest oil producer in the world, and the government played a major role in determining OPEC policy on oil production and pricing. Oil revenues were crucial to Saudi society as its economy was changed by the extraordinary wealth channeled through the government and derived from oil operations, notwithstanding a downturn in oil prices and production in the mid-1980s. Urbanization, mass public education, the presence of numerous foreign workers, and access to new media all affected Saudi values and mores. While society changed profoundly, however, political processes did not. The political elite came to include more bureaucrats and technocrats, but real power continued in the hands of the dynasty.

The Persian Gulf War and its Aftermath

Saudi political leadership was challenged when Iraq, after having rejected attempted Saudi mediation, reasserted its earlier claims and invaded neighbouring Kuwait on Aug. 2, 1990, precipitating the Persian Gulf War (1990–91). The Kuwaiti government fled to Saudi Arabia, and King Fahd denounced the Iraqi invaders. Fearing that Pres. Ṣaddām Ḥussein of Iraq might invade Saudi Arabia next (in spite of Saudi assistance to Iraq during the Iran-Iraq War), the Saudis, breaking with tradition, invited the United States and other countries to send troops to protect the kingdom.

Saudi troops defending the border with Iraq during the Persian Gulf War in 1990. Providing armed forces and a strategic launch position, Saudi Arabia was instrumental in Iraq's expulsion from Kuwait. Barry Iverson/Time & Life Pictures/Getty Images

This was done after Fahd had received the approbation of the kingdom's highest-ranking religious official, Sheikh ʿAbd al-ʿAzīz ibn Bāz, who agreed that non-Muslims could defend Islam's holiest places. By mid-November the United States had sent 230,000 troops, which were the most important part of the coalition force that ultimately included soldiers from many other countries. The Saudis adroitly coordinated Arab and Muslim contingents and also established diplomatic ties with China, the Soviet Union, and, later, Iran. King Fahd expanded his goal beyond the protection of Saudi Arabia to include the liberation of Kuwait and, if possible, the overthrow of Ṣaddām Ḥussein.

With approval from Saudi Arabia secured in advance, the coalition, with some 800,000 troops (more than 540,000 from the United States), attacked Iraq by air on Jan. 16–17, 1991. Saudi pilots flew more than 7,000 sorties and were prominent in the battles around the Saudi town of Ra's al-Khafjī. In the four-day ground war that began on February 24, Saudi troops, including the National Guard, helped defeat the Iraqis and drive them out of Kuwait. In spite of the clear military victory, the full implications of the war for Saudi Arabia were not immediately known.

Yet as time wore on, that cardinal event, in which a fellow Arab state threatened to rend years of the royal family's accomplishments asunder, seemed to be a turning point for many aspects of Saudi political, social, and economic life. A certain malaise set in, with various groups questioning the wisdom of the royal family and demanding accountability. Many citizens questioned how a regime that had spent such vast sums on defense would, in the end, be required to call on the help of non-Muslim outsiders when it felt threatened. In the internal political sphere, two opposition movements emerged, one Islamist and the other liberal and modernist, and forced Fahd to undertake several initiatives.

The economic impact of the Persian Gulf War was considerable, as Saudi Arabia housed and assisted not only foreign troops but also Kuwaiti civilians while at the same time expelling Yemenis and Jordanians, whose countries had supported Iraq diplomatically. Saudi Arabia purchased new weapons from abroad, increased the size of its own armed forces, and gave financial subsidies to a number of foreign governments. Higher Saudi oil production and substantially higher prices in the world oil market provided some compensation for the Saudi economy. The GDP per capita grew only marginally through the 1990s, however, and in real terms actually fell in some years. A languid economy—in a country perceived as otherwise being extremely wealthy—combined with a growth in unemployment to contribute to the kingdom's sense of malaise. This disquiet added to a subsequent rise in civil unrest.

One of the first results of the altered situation in Saudi Arabia was King Fahd's March 1, 1992, issuance of three important decrees: the Basic Law of Government, the Consultative Council Statute, and the Regions Statute. Whereas Fahd was responding to demands for greater governmental accountability, the first and second decrees contained a number of quasi-constitutional clauses. But since the government had often stated that the Qur'ān and the Sunnah (practices) of the Prophet were the country's constitution, he was at pains to state that there had not been a "constitutional vacuum" in Saudi Arabia and that the new laws confirmed existing practice.

The Saudi dilemma was to respond to dissent while making as few actual changes in the status quo as possible. The Basic Law of Government changed the process used to select the heir to the throne by extending candidates to the grandchildren of Ibn Saʿūd, enshrined the king's right to choose his heir, established a right to privacy, and prohibited infringements of human rights without just cause. The Consultative Council Statute set up an advisory body of 60 (later expanded to 120) members plus a chairman. While convoking a council gave the appearance of a step toward a more representative government, the council actually was appointed by the king and could be dissolved by him at will.

Fahd made it clear that he did not have democracy in mind. He was quoted as saying, "A system based on elections is not consistent with our Islamic creed, which [approves of] government by consultation [*shūrā*]."

The Islamist Opposition

After the Persian Gulf War, Saudi Arabia's Islamist opposition grew more influential. It was not made up of extremists like Juhaymān. Instead, highly educated academics and Islamic preachers from the lower ranks of the establishment ulama formed its core. It was a loose agglomeration of various trends, but the main spokesmen were two charismatic preachers, Salmān al-ʿAwdah and Safār al-Ḥawālī. Their main grievance was that the regime failed to act according to what the opposition defined as proper Islamic norms in foreign and domestic affairs. Criticism of the government was not allowed in Saudi Arabia, but in September 1992 a group associated with the two clerics published a daring, lengthy, and detailed document called the "Memorandum of Exhortation," in which they took the regime to task for having an overfinanced military that did not live up to expectations, for glorifying decadent and Westernized lifestyles, and for not allowing dissenting Islamist opinions to be expressed in print and on the airwaves.

The regime tried to rely on clerics with whom it had close ties to reign in the dissidents, but to no avail. The kingdom's first organized Sunni Islamist opposition group, the Committee for the Defense of Legitimate Rights (CDLR), was established in 1993. The committee was not a Western-style human rights organization—as its English-language sobriquet might suggest—but an Islamist opposition group that demanded that the regime act according to the strict Islamic norms on which the country had been founded. Its original members were clerics and university faculty, and it was quick to disseminate its message via telephone facsimile and, later, the Internet.

The Islamist challenge that faced the regime was an especially troubling one inasmuch as the regime itself had risen to power and maintained its status by appealing to those same Islamic symbols. This attack threatened to undermine the Saʿūd family's very legitimacy, and the family reacted by outlawing the committee and arresting its members. The group thereafter operated abroad, in London, until it split in 1996.

Meanwhile, in 1994 the first mass Islamist demonstration was held in the central Arabian city of Buraydah, following the arrest of al-Ḥawālī. It was led by al-ʿAwdah, who was arrested during the demonstration. While one could not conclude that Islamist opposition was rampant, the fact that such a large demonstration was held at all was an indication that all was not right in the capital. The demonstration was followed by a further crackdown on dissent.

The dissidents condemned the regime's supposed un-Islamic practices. Of particular concern to them was the presence of U.S. troops and those of other non-Muslim countries on Saudi soil, a presence that—given the proximity of the two holy cities—they deemed not only an affront to their religion but a situation designed only to protect the regime. In November 1995 an explosion rocked the central Riyadh headquarters of a U.S. government group that trained members of the Saudi National Guard. The explosion killed five Americans and two Indians. Three hitherto-unknown organizations took responsibility for the operation, and all of them demanded the withdrawal of U.S. forces from the kingdom. While there was no proven connection between the bombers and the known leaders of the Saudi Islamist movement, in May 1996 Saudi authorities arrested and executed four youths who claimed—in televised confessions—to have been influenced by the CDLR and by the views of an Afghanistan-based Saudi Islamist financier, Osama bin Laden.

In June 1996 a massive explosion ripped through an apartment complex housing U.S. Air Force personnel. Nineteen U.S. servicemembers were killed, and hundreds were injured. The bombing remained unsolved, but U.S. and Saudi authorities suggested that Iranian-backed Saudi Shīʿites were involved.

Although they still actively campaigned from abroad—particularly on the Internet—Islamists maintained a low profile within the kingdom throughout the 1990s. Indications were that Crown Prince ʿAbd Allāh (Abdullah)—who had effectively run day-to-day affairs after Fahd suffered a stroke in 1995—had either reached some kind of agreement with Islamist leaders or had been granted some form of grace period by them. In 1999 the government ordered the release of the opposition clerics al-Ḥawālī and al-ʿAwdah, and, although there were no indications of the conditions of their release, the two thereafter refrained from publicly criticizing the royal family.

Far more ominous was the development outside the kingdom of a network, which was associated with bin Laden, known as al-Qaeda. Although there were no direct attacks against the regime either at home or abroad, al-Qaeda staged a number of violent attacks against U.S. targets throughout the world. These attacks culminated in the September 11 terrorist attacks in 2001, a majority of whose participants were citizens of Saudi Arabia.

Foreign Policy Since the End of the Persian Gulf War

Saudi Arabia owed a tremendous debt to the countries whose forces had defeated Iraq, particularly to the United States. The kingdom repaid this debt in part by purchasing large quantities of weapons from American firms and by supporting the U.S.-led peace process between Israel and the Palestinians. In the aftermath of the war, however, the kingdom also sought to cultivate closer relations with other regional powers, particularly with Iran.

Saudi Arabia played a behind-the-scenes role in Israeli-Palestinian peace negotiations by persuading Syria to attend the October 1991 Madrid Conference, which opened the postwar peace dialogue in the region. Saudi Arabia held observer status at the conference and was active in an effort to soften Syria's position against Israel, though with little avail. Following the signing of the Oslo Accords between Israel and the Palestine Liberation Organization (PLO) in 1993, the government overcame its anger at PLO chairman Yāsir ʿArafāt for having supported Iraq during the Persian Gulf War and pledged large sums of money to support the development of the Palestinian Authority. In 1994 the Saudis, encouraged by the United States, led the Gulf Cooperation Council in withdrawing from a long-standing Arab League boycott of companies either directly or indirectly doing business with Israel.

With Iraq seemingly chastened by the Persian Gulf War, Saudi worries over regional security turned to Iran, which, since the Islamic revolution, had purportedly sought to export the revolution to other countries in the region with significant Shīʿite populations, such as Iraq, Lebanon, Bahrain, and Saudi Arabia. In strongly opposing Iran, the Saudi government also followed the U.S. policy of "dual containment" (i.e., isolating both Iran and Iraq), in which the United States sought to depict Iran as a "rogue" state that supported terrorism.

By 1996, however, Saudi Arabia's sense of obligation to the United States for its support during the war had begun to wane. Saudi leaders, particularly the newly powerful ʿAbd Allāh, began to develop closer relations with Iran. ʿAbd Allāh, keen to put a distance between his policies and the unpopular pro-Western policies of Fahd, apparently assessed that the United States would continue to support the Saʿūd family, in spite of U.S. antipathy toward Iran, and so turned his attention to improving regional relations. Soon dignitaries from Iran and Saudi Arabia were exchanging visits, and the two countries' leaders were cooperating in several matters. The kingdom also resolved several long-standing border disputes. These actions included significantly reshaping its border with Yemen.

In the end, however, the greatest hurdle to U.S.-Saudi relations came from within the kingdom—from the Saudi citizens who participated in the September 11 attacks and other acts of terrorism against the United States. The perception of many Americans was that the royal family, through its long and close relations with the Wahhābī sect, had laid the groundwork for the growth of militant groups like al-Qaeda and that after the attacks had done little to help track the militants or ward off future atrocities. That viewpoint was reinforced when in 2003 the Saudi government refused to support or to participate in the Iraq War between U.S.-led forces and Iraq, an action seen by some as an attempt by the royal family to placate the kingdom's Islamist radicals. That same year Saudi and U.S. government officials agreed to withdraw all U.S. military forces from Saudi soil. In December 2005 Saudi Arabia formally joined the World Trade Organization.

King ʿAbd Allāh, the reigning monarch of Saudi Arabia, in a photo taken in 2005. Hassan Ammar/AFP/Getty Images

Reign of King ʿAbd Allāh from 2005

The country underwent a peaceful power transition in 2005, when, following Fahd's death on August 1, ʿAbd Allāh ascended the throne. The new king subsequently introduced a program of moderate reform to address a number of challenges facing Saudi Arabia. The country's continued reliance on oil revenue was of particular concern, and among the economic reforms he introduced were limited deregulation, foreign investment, and privatization. He originally sought to placate extreme Islamist voices—many of which sought to end the Saʿūdī dynasty's rule—yet the spectre of anti-Saudi and anti-Western violence within the country's borders led him for the first time to order the use of force by the security services against some extremists. At the same time, in 2005 ʿAbd Allāh responded to demands for greater political inclusiveness by holding the country's first municipal elections, based on adult male suffrage.

Uncertainty surrounding succession in the kingdom was a further source of domestic concern, and late the following year ʿAbd Allāh issued a new law refining the country's succession policies. Among the changes was the establishment of an Allegiance Commission, a council of Saudi princes meant to participate in the selection of a crown prince—previously the task of the king alone—and to oversee a smooth transition of power. In February 2009 ʿAbd Allāh enacted a series of broad governmental changes, which affected areas such as the judiciary, armed forces, and various ministries. Notable among his decisions were the replacement of senior individuals within the judiciary and the religious police with more moderate candidates and the appointment of the country's first female deputy minister, who was charged with overseeing girls' education.

CHAPTER 6

Yemen: The Land and its People

Yemen is bounded to the north by Saudi Arabia, to the east by Oman, to the south by the Gulf of Aden and the Arabian Sea, and to the west by the Red Sea. Most of Yemen's northern frontier with Saudi Arabia traverses the great desert of the peninsula, the Rubʿ al-Khali ("Empty Quarter"), and until 2000 remained undemarcated, as did the eastern frontier with Oman until 1992. Yemen's territory includes a number of islands as well, including the Kamarān group, located in the Red Sea near Al-Ḥudaydah; the Ḥanīsh Islands, in the southern Red Sea; Perim (Barīm) Island, in the Bab el-Mandeb Strait, which separates the Arabian Peninsula from Africa; Socotra (Suquṭrā), Yemen's most important and largest island, located in the Arabian Sea nearly 620 miles (1,000 km) east of Aden; and the Brothers (Al-Ikhwān), a group of small islets near Socotra.

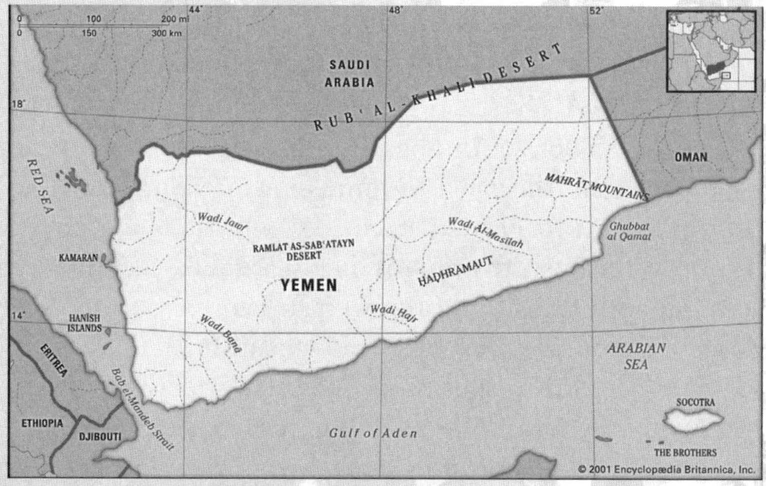

Yemen. Encyclopaedia Britannica, Inc.

Yemen is an overwhelmingly rural country, and the majority of the rural Yemeni population is distributed rather evenly. Sanaa, the capital, is by far the largest city. The Yemeni population is overwhelmingly Arab, and they have tended to divide themselves into northern and southern groups (the division is a historical one with linguistic roots, but it is otherwise obscure). Tribal affiliation is an important component of Yemeni Arab society, and some confederations have histories some 2,000 years in length. Tribal affiliation continues to inform Yemeni social and political life, although efforts have been made to diminish its influence. Yemen's ethnic minorities include the Mahra, a group whose roots are unclear; the Akhdām, who form a distinct social group unto themselves; and Ethiopian and Somali communities that have migrated to Yemen over the course of many centuries.

RELIEF AND DRAINAGE

Yemen may be divided into five major regions: a coastal plain running north-south known as the Tihāmah (an extension of the Tihāmat ʿAsīr); the western highlands; the central mountains (the Yemen Highlands); the eastern highlands; and, finally, the eastern and northeastern desert regions.

The coastal plain ranges in width from 5 miles (8 km) to as much as 40 miles (65 km). Low mountains rising from 1,000 to 3,500 feet (300 to 1,100 m) lie between the low hills of the plain and the great central massif, which has many peaks in excess of 10,000 feet (3,000 m); the highest is Mount Al-Nabī Shuʿayb, which rises to 12,336 feet (3,760 m). Toward the east-northeast, the mountains subside rather rapidly into the eastern highlands

(2,500–3,500 feet [750–1,100 m]), which drop off to the sandy hills of the Rub' al-Khali.

Yemen is an arid country, and there are no permanent watercourses. The regular precipitation that occurs in some areas drains, in the northern part, westward toward the Red Sea through five major watercourses (wadis) and, in the southern part, southward into the Gulf of Aden and the Arabian Sea through three major watercourses. The largest of the latter is the Wadi Ḥaḍramawt (Hadhramaut Valley), which has been renowned since antiquity for its frankincense trees and which historically has been the locus of a number of sophisticated city-states. Together with their tributaries and lesser neighbours, these intermittently flowing channels slice the highlands and central massif into a large number of plateaus and ridges.

In many places there is evidence of volcanic activity from as recently as a few hundred years ago. The existence of hot springs and fumaroles (volcanic vents) attests to continued subterranean activity. Moreover, the country sits astride one of the most active fault lines in the Red Sea region (Great Rift Basin) and has experienced several severe earthquakes in modern times, including one that shook the Dhamār area in December 1982, killing about 3,000 people and largely destroying several villages and hundreds of smaller settlements.

Soils throughout the country vary from sandy to loamy, and most are low in organic matter, thus limiting agricultural options. In some areas, however, elaborate agricultural terraces cover the mountains from base to peak. The high agricultural productivity of this system is largely attributable to the soil that has been collected and enriched with compost over a period of centuries. In the modern period, neglect and civil conflict have taken their toll on the earthworks, which are particularly vulnerable to erosion. Still, the terraces are largely intact and are a breathtaking feature of mountainous Yemen.

CLIMATE

Most of Yemen lies in the border zone between two main weather patterns: the regular northerly winds (from the Mediterranean basin) and the southwest monsoon winds. These create a fairly well-defined seasonal rhythm; the northerly winds predominate during the winter, while in the summer, the southwest monsoon brings the primary rains. Cut off from this pattern by the central mountains, the southern fringe areas on the Gulf of Aden experience a markedly tropical climate. In Aden as well as in the north at Al-Ḥudaydah, temperatures often reach the 100s F (upper 30s C), with high humidity, whereas in Sanaa (at more than 7,200 feet [2,200 m]) the daytime temperature averages in the upper 60s F (low 20s C), and humidity is low. The higher northern elevations of the central massif experience occasional frosts and dustings of snow during the winter months.

On the Tihāmah, as well as along the southern coastal belt, the average annual precipitation is less than about 5 inches (130 mm); many years record no measurable precipitation. Precipitation increases with elevation; the lower highlands receive about 15 to 20 inches (400 to 500 mm) per year, while the middle highlands around Taʿizz and Ibb average more than 30 inches (750 mm) annually. Different annual cycles characterize the northern and southern parts of Yemen: whereas the north usually has two rainy seasons (March–May and July–September), the south often receives no precipitation except sparse amounts in the summer months. Throughout Yemen, precipitation is erratic and variable from year to year, and lengthy droughts are not unknown. There have been periods as long as five years when precipitation was one-tenth the normal amount. A serious drought occurred during North Yemen's civil war of 1962–70 and had lasting social and economic consequences.

PLANT AND ANIMAL LIFE

The distribution of vegetation roughly corresponds to the zones of elevation and precipitation. It is possible to distinguish three general regions: (1) the coastal plain and its wadis, in which dry-climate plants such as the date palm, citrus fruits, banana, and cotton as well as spurges (euphorbia), acacia, and tamarisk predominate (the dry wadis of the eastern desert support similar flora), (2) the middle highlands, with a variety of such food crops as melons, nuts, grapes, and grains, as well as various spurges, eucalyptus, sycamore, fig, and carob, and (3) the mountainous interior, with its temperate-zone crops, including coffee, the mild stimulant khat (*qāt*), and a variety of woody shrubs and trees. Yemen retained considerable forest cover into the early years of the 20th century. However, the pressures generated by rapid population growth—notably the increased demand for stovewood and agricultural land—largely depleted the forest legacy. In the early 21st century a negligible amount of forest cover remained.

These same human pressures have had a devastating effect on Yemen's wildlife. Evidence suggests the presence of such species as panther, ostrich, various antelopes (including the Arabian oryx), and large cats (e.g., lions) as recently as a century ago. Some species of panther and antelope, which persist in Yemen, are threatened, surviving in limited numbers. One of the largest wild mammals still widespread in Yemen is the hamadryas baboon (*Papio*

Arabian oryx (Oryx leucoryx). Rod Moon—The National Audubon Society Collection/Photo Researchers

hamadryas), though its numbers too are said to be diminished. Among the smaller mammals are the hyena, fox, and rabbit. In two categories of wildlife—birds and insects—Yemen has a relatively abundant and varied population; many species remain uncatalogued. Probably the greatest diversity of fauna, however, inhabits the waters of the Red Sea, the Arabian Sea, and the Gulf of Aden. Among the many different species are tuna, mackerel, shark, sardines, lobster, shrimp, and squid.

ETHNIC GROUPS

The people of Yemen overwhelmingly consider themselves Arabs, but they have tended to divide themselves between northern and southern groups, a historical division that has linguistic roots but which is otherwise difficult to trace. Yemenis of northern origin, for example, are said to have descended from Mesopotamians who entered the region in the 1st millennium BCE, and they claim ancestry of the biblical figure Ismāʿīl (Ishmael). The southern group, which represents the old South Arabian heritage, claims descent from Qaḥṭān, the biblical Joktan.

Ethnic minorities include the Mahra, a people whose roots are unclear and who occupy a part of eastern Yemen, as well as the island of Socotra, and who speak a variant of the ancient Himyaritic language. On the Tihāmah coastal plain, in-migrations from Ethiopia and Somalia have occurred over many centuries. There is a clear African admixture in the coastal population as well as a distinct social group known as the Akhdām, who perform menial tasks and are the closest thing to a caste in Yemen. In the far north there are still small remnants of the once-large Jewish communities (most migrated to Israel after 1948), while in the area of Aden and the eastern regions there are distinct Somali, Indonesian, and Indian elements in the population, legacies of the British colonial era as well of economic and political ties extending back over two millennia.

Among Arab groups, tribal affiliation is another deep-seated component of social identity. Some tribal confederations have histories spanning more than two millennia. These affiliations continue to serve as a key basis for political and social organization throughout the country, although the postindependence governments of both South Yemen and, to a lesser extent, North Yemen set out to eradicate what then were considered reactionary cultural institutions. Although efforts toward detribalization were at least in part effective, subsequent events indicated that such identifications were still socially, economically, and politically relevant.

LANGUAGES

More than nine-tenths of Yemenis speak some dialect of Arabic as their first language, and Modern Standard Arabic—the literary and cultural language of the broader Arab world—is taught in schools. There are several main dialects, but minor differences often occur within smaller geographic areas. The Arabic of the rural areas of the south is still heavily influenced by the ancient South Arabian languages. A dialect of Judeo-Arabic spoken by the Jewish community has fallen almost entirely out of use in Yemen. Hindi, Somali, and several African languages are spoken in pockets. Several ancient Semitic dialects, including Bathari, Mehri, and Socotri (Soqotri), remain in a chiefly oral capacity. Those languages have tended to recede as literacy in Arabic has become more common.

RELIGION

Throughout society, the broadest distinctions between population groups are based not on ethnicity but on religious affiliation. Islam is the state religion, and the Sunni branch of Islam, represented by the Shāfiʿī school, predominates. The Shīʿite minority consists of the Zaydī school, which has long been politically dominant in the mountainous highlands of the north, and the Ismāʿīlīs, now a relatively small group found in the Haraz region of northern Yemen and in Jabal Manakhah, the mountainous area west of Sanaa. The non-Muslim community is very small, consisting mostly of foreign visitors and workers. All are free to worship as they wish—including the Jewish community—but, as in most conservative Muslim countries, proselytizing of Muslims by non-Muslims is illegal.

Historically, Yemen has had its share of Islamic militants, particularly since the return of combatants who fought in the 1980s on the side of the mujahideen (Arabic: *mujāhidūn*, "those who engage in jihad") in the Afghan War (1978–92).

Zaydiyyah

The sect of Shīʿite Muslims owing allegiance to Zayd ibn ʿAlī, grandson of Ḥusayn ibn ʿAlī, is collectively known as the Zaydiyyah. Doctrinally the Zaydiyyah are closer to the majority Sunnis than are the other Shīʿites. Early in the 10th century the Zaydiyyah became dominant in Yemen, and thereafter Zaydī imams were the spiritual rulers of that area. From the departure of the Turks in 1917 until 1962, they were also the temporal rulers of Yemen.

SETTLEMENT PATTERNS

Yemen is an overwhelmingly rural country, with more than two-thirds of the people living in the countryside. With only a few exceptions, the rural population is distributed fairly evenly. The monsoon precipitation that causes the western slopes of the massif to be so well-dissected makes the area the most densely populated part of the country. Fertile soils are another regional asset. In varying concentrations, Yemenis inhabit nearly all the country's geographic zones—from sea level to 10,000 feet (3,000 m) and higher. (In fact, the intricate variety of subregions and microclimates produces an agricultural base of astonishing diversity.) The scarcity of farmland has greatly influenced rural settlement and construction patterns, as has the need for security.

Villages tend to be small, and buildings are erected on ground that cannot be cultivated—frequently along cliffs and rock outcroppings. Homes often consist of several stories (as many as five or more), with the lower floors being made of hand-hewn stone. Upper stories, where the family resides, are usually made of mud brick, a superior insulator. These quarters also have many windows, providing ventilation in the heat of the summer. The location of the living quarters in these upper stories offers the capacity for storage in the lower stories, as well as an element of security.

Cities in Yemen follow patterns seen in other parts of the Arab world. Original construction consisted of a walled and fortified old city, in which the ornate multistory home was standard. The old city also contained shops, souks, schools, and mosques. In the modern period, urban areas began to sprawl outside the old city, and the wealthy began to build larger and more-ornate mansions and villas in nearby suburbs.

A neighbourhood in western Sanaa, Yemen. Art Resource, New York

DEMOGRAPHIC TRENDS

In many respects, the most important contemporary demographic trend has been the emigration of large numbers of males between the ages of 15 and 45 for employment in other countries. The number of such emigrants has fluctuated because of political and economic volatility over the years. Until the last decade of the 20th century, there were more than one million Yemeni nationals employed abroad—chiefly in Saudi Arabia and the smaller Arab countries of the Persian Gulf region, as well as in Great Britain (in the industrial Midlands and in Wales), and in the United States (in industrial areas of the Northeast and Midwest and in the agricultural areas of California). The remittances of these emigrants played an important role in the balance of payments, in radically increasing the income of most Yemenis, and in funding many local development projects. Iraq's invasion of Kuwait in 1990, however, drastically altered the balance of migrant labour. Yemen's neutrality and failure to support a U.S.-Saudi military coalition against Iraq resulted in Saudi Arabia's retraction of the special status granted to Yemeni workers. As many as one million labourers were forced to return to a newly unified Yemen that was ill-prepared to reabsorb them.

The population of Yemen continues to display characteristics typical of less-developed areas: high birth rate, high infant mortality rate, low levels of literacy, and the ill effects of poor hygiene, unsanitary water supplies, and inadequate public health service. Major health and education programs funded by foreign governments and by the United Nations have attempted to address both structural and programmatic deficiencies.

CHAPTER 7

The Yemeni Economy

In spite of economic advances since the 1970s—most notably the beginning of the commercial exploitation of oil and natural gas—Yemen is one of the world's poorest and least-developed countries. The majority of Yemenis are subsistence agriculturalists. Only about 3 percent of the country's land is arable (mostly in the west), though roughly one-third is suitable for grazing. During the first half of the 20th century, the rulers in the north (the imams) achieved and maintained virtual self-sufficiency in food production for their region.

By contrast, at the beginning of the 21st century, unified Yemen was heavily dependent on imported food, in spite of the market expansion and increased investment of the 1970s and '80s. One important reason for this situation was the scarcity and high cost of domestic labour, the result of the exodus of much of the adult male labour force that began in the 1970s. In addition, the remittances of these emigrants (most of which were transferred through unofficial channels and therefore not taxed) fueled inflation, driving the prices of domestic food products above those of imported equivalents, such as U.S. grains and Australian meats.

One of the more important issues raised by the merger of the two Yemens was the integration of the socialist command economy of the south and the largely market-driven economy of the north. By the early 1970s the government of the south had nationalized almost all land and housing, along with most banking, industrial, and other business enterprises in the country. Thereafter, all new industries and businesses of any size were state-owned and state-operated. The private sector has since been encouraged and has been fueled by remittances from migrant workers.

Following the 1994 civil war, the regime of Col. 'Alī 'Abd Allāh Ṣāliḥ negotiated an agreement with the International Monetary Fund (IMF) and the World Bank that committed Yemen to a multiyear matrix of structural adjustments in exchange for financial and economic incentives. The package of reforms and aid, which were to be phased in over several years, was designed to make Yemen both economically viable in a postremittance era and more attractive to foreign investors in an increasingly globalized international economy. The reforms, which included the elimination of subsidies on many basic necessities, cuts in budget deficits, and the downsizing of the government and the public sector, were painful for many and generated widespread discontent and public protest; safety-net projects cushioned the economic blows for only some of the most vulnerable Yemenis, and instances of corruption and favouritism only made the sacrifices harder to accept.

Nevertheless, the regime managed to keep quite close to the schedule of reforms in the second half of the 1990s, and the IMF and World Bank repeatedly acknowledged its successes. The opening of Aden's new container port in 1999 and the ongoing development of an industrial free zone there, inaugurated in 1991, raised hopes for future economic gains.

AGRICULTURE, FORESTRY, AND FISHING

Yemen's difficult terrain, limited soil, inconsistent water supply, and large number of microclimates have fostered some of the most highly sophisticated methods of water conservation and seed adaptation found anywhere in the world, making possible the cultivation of surprisingly diverse crops. The most common crops are cereals such as millet, corn (maize), wheat, barley, and sorghum. Myriad vegetables from a burgeoning truck farm industry have appeared on the market in recent years. There has also been extensive cultivation of fruits—both tropical (mangoes, plantains, bananas, melons, papayas, and citrus) and temperate (pears, peaches, apples, and grapes).

The two main cash crops in the northern highlands are coffee (*Coffea arabica*) and khat (*qāt*; *Catha edulis*). The coffee trade, which began in the 16th century, was originally based on Yemeni coffee, and, for centuries, coffee was the most important and renowned export of Yemen. The port city of Mocha (Al-Mukhā)—from which a distinctive style of coffee takes its name—was the point from which most of Yemen's coffee was exported between the 16th and 18th centuries, before more-economical plantation cultivation was introduced in other parts of the world.

Mocha

Mocha (Arabic: Al-Mukhā) is a town in southwestern Yemen on the Red Sea and the Tihāmah coastal plain. Mocha lies at the head of a shallow bay between two headlands, with an unprotected anchorage 1.5 miles (2.5 km) offshore. Yemen's most renowned historic port, Mocha was long famous as Arabia's chief coffee-exporting centre. The term *mocha* and variations of the word have entered European languages as a synonym for the high-quality coffee of the species *Coffea arabica*, still grown in the Yemen highlands and formerly exported through the town.

Mocha's founding is traditionally associated with the Muslim mystic Sheikh ʿAlī ibn ʿUmar al-Shādhilī, who is supposed to have introduced coffee drinking to Arabia. Mocha was regularly visited by Indian traders, who traded finished metal products and textiles for Yemeni coffee and myrrh. It also dealt with Egyptian merchants, who sailed to Mocha on the summer northwesterly Red Sea winds.

Yemen came under Ottoman suzerainty in the early 16th century, and by 1600, Mocha—from which much of the region's valuable coffee export was shipped—was Yemen's most important commercial centre. Trading establishments (known as factories because they were headed by commercial agents, or factors) were maintained in Mocha by the British, the Dutch, and, briefly, the Danes and the French.

In 1636 Mocha was surrendered by the Ottomans to the Yemeni imam al-Muʾayyad Muḥammad ibn al-Qāsim. It prospered in the 17th and 18th centuries, and the Ottomans held the town again from 1849 to 1918. The conflicts between the European powers and the Ottoman Empire, and those between the Ottoman Empire and the imams of Yemen, contributed to the port's decline, which was hastened by the development of coffee plantations elsewhere in the early 18th century. The British moved their base of regional operations from Mocha to Aden in 1839 and were followed by the other European trading countries. Yemen's trade thereafter was diverted either to Aden or to Al-Ḥudaydah.

Today, most of Mocha's formerly fine public buildings, residences, and mosques are in ruins. Mocha is on a sandy, arid stretch of the coast, and blowing sand and inadequate water supply have contributed to its decline. It is the coastal terminus of a modern road (completed 1965), built partly with U.S. aid, leading eastward to Taʿizz, thence north, via Ibb and Dhamār, to the city of Sanaa, the national capital.

In Yemen the coffee tree grows best in the middle highlands, at elevations of 4,500 to 6,500 feet (1,400 to 2,000 m), where khat also flourishes. The latter is an evergreen shrub whose young leaves, which contain an alkaloid, are chewed as a mild stimulant. The production and consumption of khat occupy a prominent position in the culture and economy of Yemen. Increased affluence has allowed a growing section of the population to indulge in its use, which the government has attempted—with little success—to discourage. Greater demand has fueled a substantial increase in khat acreage. Although older coffee terraces are often converted to khat as their productivity declines, much of the land being devoted to khat was formerly considered marginal for commercial agricultural purposes and now benefits from regular soil-enhancement programs and terrace-maintenance efforts.

Beginning in the 1970s, the cultivation of cotton—both in the Tihāmah coastal plain in the north and in the coastal plain east of Aden—was strongly supported by the respective national governments, and for a while it contributed significantly to national income. At the end of the 20th century, a significant decline in world cotton prices, as well as the high costs of initiation and development, meant that the Yemeni cotton industry was not competitive.

The typical Yemeni farmer raises at least some poultry and livestock, typically regional varieties of chickens, goats, sheep, or cattle. Agricultural aid programs sponsored by Western countries in the 1970s and '80s introduced new varieties of dairy and beef cattle in the more temperate regions of the north, but Yemen still imports much of the livestock and dairy and poultry products it consumes.

Another important economic development has been the growth of both the artisanal and the industrial fishing industries. The waters of the Arabian Sea, the Red Sea, and the Gulf of Aden are extraordinarily rich in a wide variety of commercially desirable fish and crustaceans. In the past, very small quantities of some species were marketed locally. The foreign technical and financial assistance provided to the fishing industry (notably by the Soviet Union) contributed markedly to its increased role in the national economy. At the beginning of the 21st century, the developing fishery sector, also increasingly supported by domestic government programs and foreign assistance, was a major and growing contributor to Yemen's economy.

RESOURCES AND POWER

The export of oil generates a major portion of national income and government revenues. Oil and natural gas were first discovered in commercial quantity in North Yemen on the edge of the eastern desert near Ma'rib in 1984 by the Hunt Oil Company. Two years later, oil was found by a state corporation of the Soviet Union in the south, near the juncture of the two Yemens and Saudi Arabia. Since then, several other significant finds have been made, most notably the major commercial strike in 1991 in Masīlah, north of Al-Mukallā, by Canadian Occidental (later known as Nexen Inc.); the Masīlah field is one of Yemen's most productive. New exploration and the development of existing finds by several foreign companies continued in the early 21st century. Pipelines in Yemen carry crude oil to export facilities on the Red Sea, the Gulf of Aden, and the Arabian Sea.

As important, if not more so, are Yemen's large proven reserves of natural gas, located mostly in the western part of the country. Yemen has signed agreements with foreign companies to begin full exploitation of natural gas, but in the early 21st century the sector remained underdeveloped, and production was limited. Electricity is mostly generated by oil-burning thermal plants. At the end of the 20th and the beginning of the 21st century, energy restructuring plans provided for the construction of a number of gas-powered plants, with hopes that switching from oil to natural gas as Yemen's principal fuel for meeting electric and other domestic needs would maximize oil available for export and relieve domestic Yemeni oil dependence. Installed electrical capacity does not meet national demands, and scheduled blackouts are common. In the first decade of the 21st century only about two-fifths of the country was tied into the national grid.

There has never been a thorough survey of Yemen to determine precisely what other mineral resources might be commercially exploitable. Salt is extracted from underground mines near Al-Ṣalīf in the Tihāmah and from surface deposits near Aden in the south. In the past, coal and iron deposits supported a small-scale steel industry (primarily for the manufacture of swords and daggers, particularly the *janbiyyah*, a symbolic, largely ornamental dagger worn by many Yemeni men). There are deposits of copper, as well as some evidence of sulfur, lead, zinc, nickel, silver, and gold, and surveys in the late 20th and early 21st centuries indicated that some of these deposits were commercially exploitable.

MANUFACTURING

Continuing today in Yemen are traditional handicraft industries that achieved great renown in the past for the quality of their products: jewelry, especially silver and gold filigree; leatherwork; carpets; glass; utensils, especially for cooking; daggers and other metalwork; decorative woodwork; and stained-glass windows. Modern manufacturing enterprises did not contribute to the national income

A Yemeni woman oversees the machinery at a textile plant. The textile industry is one of the modern industries developed in Yemen after the 1960s. Steven L. Raymer/National Geographic Image Collection/Getty Images

until the 1970s, with the exceptions of the oil refinery in Little Aden (the peninsula that encloses the western side of Aden's harbour), built originally by British Petroleum in the 1950s and nationalized in 1977, and the cotton textile industry established in North Yemen in the last years of the imamate at the beginning of the 1960s.

The multiyear development plans of the governments of both Yemens after the 1960s focused on the establishment of a more diversified and modern industrial base. Most of these manufacturers were designed as import-substitution enterprises, producing such items as cement, aluminum ware, plastic products, paints, textiles, furniture, cooking oil, foodstuffs, soft drinks, and tobacco products. Some have since become significant contributors to the national income. Much of new manufacturing in recent decades has been related to transportation and communications infrastructure: road building, the construction of electrical power stations, electrification, and the stringing of telephone lines. The oil and natural gas industry entails—in addition to the foreign primary firms—an array of local subcontractors and allied services. Pipeline construction and maintenance, as well as new refineries, make substantial contributions to the economy.

FINANCE

The Central Bank of Yemen was formed in 1990 from the merger of the central banks of the two Yemens. It is responsible for issuing the rial, the national currency, and for managing the government's foreign exchange and other financial operations. The Yemen Bank for Reconstruction and Development (1962) provides commercial and customer services. Banking is a small sector of the economy. Services have traditionally been difficult to obtain since, because of a weak court system, collecting money owed has been difficult. Many Yemenis rely on informal systems to meet financial needs.

TRADE

For many centuries, trade was the major source of wealth for the states that occupied the southern corner of the Arabian Peninsula. Trade diminished in the 16th century, when the Portuguese set out to control seaborne commerce with the East, turning the Red Sea region, and especially Yemen, into an economic backwater. The only world commodity left to Yemen was the coffee trade, a monopoly that continued for several centuries. The construction of the Suez Canal (completed in 1869) revitalized the Red Sea route between Asia and Europe, proving prescient the British decision to take Aden in 1839. Aden's deepwater berths and sophisticated and extensive port facilities, which the British constructed over the years, made it one of the world's preeminent ports.

Still, trade remained quite modest until the economic boom of the 1970s and '80s; at the height of this boom, the value of Yemeni exports (primarily coffee, cotton goods, and hides and skins) amounted to only a minute fraction of imports, which comprised foodstuffs of all types, manufactured goods (consumer as well as industrial), machinery, transportation equipment, chemicals, and petroleum products—the basic goods demanded by a population formerly isolated from the modern consumer economy. The ratio of exports to imports began to shift dramatically with the start of the export of oil in the late 1980s. With the exception of oil exports, however, Yemen conducts all but an infinitesimal portion of its export trade with its regional neighbours.

SERVICES

Within the service sector, public administration is one of the largest employers. Overall, the service sector accounts for a significant proportion of the gross domestic product (GDP), although it does not employ a large proportion of the labour force. Tourism accounts for a relatively small portion of the GDP. In spite of Yemen's rich natural and cultural heritage and government efforts to encourage tourism, the infrastructural underdevelopment and political instability have made many visitors wary of travel to the country.

LABOUR AND TAXATION

Although the government acknowledges the right of workers to organize, union membership in Yemen is minimal. All unions are federated within an umbrella labour organization, the General Federation of Trade Unions of Yemen. Collective bargaining is limited, and work stoppages and strikes are permitted only with government approval. A significant proportion of Yemen's workforce is engaged in agricultural labour. Unemployment frequently exceeds 30 percent. Child labour is common, particularly in agriculture, and laws limiting the work hours of children under age 15 are seldom enforced. As in some other Muslim countries, the standard workweek is Saturday through Wednesday.

The country derives some one-fifth of its income from tax revenue, of which taxes derived from the oil industry are the most significant. There is a personal income tax, and income derived from tariffs and other taxation has traditionally been a major source of the state's non-petroleum-based income. The Islamic tithe (*zakāt*) is administered by the state (though calculated by the individual); the proceeds are intended for the relief of the poor. Before 2000 the undemarcated frontier with Saudi Arabia, as well as the fluid political situation along those portions of the frontier that were demarcated (e.g., near Najrān, Saudi Arabia), made smuggling—and thus the loss of much-needed import duties—a chronic problem for revenue collectors.

TRANSPORTATION AND TELECOMMUNICATIONS

Until the 1960s there were virtually no all-weather roads anywhere in Yemen except in the city of Aden. In the last years of the imamate, the first of these roads were built in the north as part of foreign-aid packages by China, the United States, and the Soviet Union. These first roads—i.e., the one from Al-Ḥudaydah to Sanaa and the one from Mocha to Sanaa via Taʿizz—represented major feats of engineering. They cut the transportation time between the cities involved from days to hours and set off an explosion of intrastate traffic and trade.

Since then, many of the formerly rudimentary roads in the north and south have been paved, and demands for similar improvements have been raised by numerous small towns and villages. Although all the major towns and cities are now served by all-weather roads, there are thousands of miles of tracks that are passable only by all-terrain vehicles. Built at an accelerated rate since the mid-1970s, these tracks have provided an outlet for locally produced goods and easier access to consumer products. The former capital cities of Aden and Sanaa remain the transportation hubs of the south and north, respectively, and travel between most of the lesser towns and cities is not possible except through these centres.

The 1970s and '80s saw the development of a public transportation system based on buses and shared taxis.

Armoured army cars driving through the rugged Yemeni terrain. Many sections of the country do not have paved roads but, rather, dirt-and-stone tracks that are navigable only by all-terrain vehicles. AFP/Getty Images

Beginning in the late 20th century, the distribution of goods has been handled primarily by modern trucks, some of immense size; these trucks are often overloaded, and the accident rate on Yemeni roads is disproportionately high.

Until the early 1960s, about three-fourths of North Yemen's very modest international trade passed through Aden. Following the revolution of 1962, however, the new government redirected trade through the Red Sea port of Al-Ḥudaydah, which was expanded and modernized with major assistance from the Soviet Union. The ports of Aden and Al-Ḥudaydah now handle nearly all of Yemen's sea traffic. Although Al-Ḥudaydah's port is well-equipped, it has experienced periods of serious congestion. Aden's extensive facilities were underutilized during the socialist period. With unification and the major upgrading of port and manufacturing facilities that began in the late

20th century (including the inauguration of an industrial free zone in 1991 and the opening of a container port in 1999), Aden—which has good road connections to Taʿizz, Ibb, and beyond—will have the ability to handle most of the country's international trade. Yemen's other ports, most notably Mocha and Al-Mukallā, used chiefly by small craft and for coastal traffic and, in the case of Mocha, for smuggling, began plans for revival in the late 20th century. While Mocha canceled most of its development plans after Yemen's unification, in the early 21st century Al-Mukallā was included in a development program designed to expand the infrastructure of three of Yemen's port cities.

Prior to unification, the state-owned airlines of the two Yemens provided each country with its chief transport link to the outside world for passengers, mail, and light freight. Both airlines, but especially the one in the south, greatly facilitated internal travel and transport between the cities and major towns of Yemen. The two airlines were finally merged nearly a decade after unification. Today, Yemenia (Yemen Airways) operates regular service to a large number of countries in the Red Sea region and to most other Arab states, as well as to a growing number of European transportation hubs. Major airports are at Aden, Sanaa, and Al-Ḥudaydah. There are a number of other smaller airports and airfields located in other cities.

There are relatively few main phone lines in Yemen, and, like many other less-developed countries, Yemen is experiencing a boom in cellular and wireless phone service, with such service being provided by several private companies. The number of televisions and radios per capita is quite high. Television and radio stations are located in the larger cities, and more-affluent Yemenis have access to satellite feeds from other Arab countries and elsewhere. Internet service is modest but increasing, and few people own computers.

Al-Ḥudaydah

Al-Ḥudaydah (also spelled Hodeida) is situated on the Tihāmah coastal plain that borders the Red Sea in western Yemen and is one of the country's chief ports. Al-Ḥudaydah was first mentioned in Islamic chronicles in 1454/55 and was long overshadowed by the port town of Mocha, a major coffee transshipment centre. In later centuries, however, both Al-Ḥudaydah and Aden superseded Mocha in importance. While under Ottoman suzerainty, Al-Ḥudaydah was the landing site for successive Ottoman attempts to wrest full control of Yemen from its traditional rulers. During the Italo-Turkish War of 1911–12 the city was shelled by Italian warships lying offshore. After World War I the victorious British handed over Al-Ḥudaydah to the Idrīsī rulers of Asir, to the north, but the area was retaken by Imam Yaḥyā Maḥmūd al-Mutawakkil in 1925. A Yemeni-fomented revolt in Asir (by then part of Saudi Arabia) in 1934 led to Saudi occupation of Al-Ḥudaydah. The Treaty of Al-Ṭā'if of that year returned the city and the Yemeni Tihāmah to Yemen; the latter, in turn, recognized Saudi Arabia's possession of Asir. The city was seat of a semiautonomous administration under one of the Yemeni imam's sons until proclamation of the republic and the subsequent civil war (1962–70).

A radical change in the city's economic life took place after 1961, when the Soviet Union completed construction of the deep-water port several miles north. The port, with modern facilities for ships drawing up to 26 feet (8 m) of water, was built in the lagoon of Al-Kathīb Bay and was protected from winds by a hook-shaped spit that culminated in Cape Al-Kathīb. The old port at the city site was an open roadstead; ships had to unload their cargoes into small dhows and lighters. Grain silos were constructed in the new port for the secure storage of grain supplies for the population. Another factor in the city's development was the opening of an all-weather improved road from there to Sanaa, the country's capital; another new road, to the inland city of Taʿizz, was also built. In the early 21st century, Al-Ḥudaydah was Yemen's main Red Sea port and the site of one of the country's major airports.

CHAPTER 8

Yemeni Government and Society

The former states of North Yemen and South Yemen had sharply contrasting political systems. North Yemen was a republic governed nominally under a constitution adopted in 1970, suspended in 1974, and largely restored between 1978 and the late 1980s. Although a succession of bodies carried out some of the functions of a legislature, they exercised little real power until the late 1980s. During that period, policy making remained in the hands of a relatively progressive military elite that worked closely with a variety of civilians that included a large and growing group of technocrats, the major tribal leaders, and other traditional conservative notables. Although political parties were formally banned, several parties did exist and operated with varying degrees of influence during and between elections.

South Yemen, also republican in form, had an avowedly Marxist regime, and the political system and economy reflected many of the goals and organizational structures of its "scientific socialism." The Yemen Socialist Party (YSP), the only legal political organization, determined government policy and exercised control over the state administrative system, the legislature, and the military.

The unified political system created in 1990 represented a pronounced departure from either of the previous ones, in theory and, to a large extent, in practice. The most important change was the decision to establish a multiparty representative democracy.

Constitutional Framework

The 1990 constitution (amended in 1994 and 2001) called for those rights and institutions usually associated with a liberal parliamentary democracy. The head of state is the president, who appoints the vice president and the prime minister; the latter is the head of government. The president, elected by direct popular vote, holds office for no more than two seven-year terms and is assisted by a cabinet.

The bicameral legislature consists of two houses: the House of Representatives, whose members are elected by universal adult suffrage every six years, and the Shūrā (Consultative) Council, whose members are appointed by the president. The legislature oversees the executive, discusses and drafts legislation, and authorizes government budgets and economic plans. The constitution may be modified with a two-thirds vote by the House of Representatives.

Members of the Yemeni House of Representatives take a vote in 2008. Khaled Fazaa/AFP/Getty Images

LOCAL GOVERNMENT

The issue of redefining territorial and administrative subdivisions after union was complex. In the north the provinces had corresponded to more or less obvious topographical regions. Each province was subdivided into *qaḍāʾ* (district) and *nāḥiyah* (tract) levels, largely representing distinctions within the population (e.g., tribal affiliations). In the south, under the British, there had been a major distinction regarding administrative autonomy and political influence between the city of Aden (governed directly from London via the colonial office) and the hinterland, which was divided into more than 20 "statelets," many of which were clearly associated with ancient tribal groupings of one form or another. In order to break down the old tribal affiliations and the associated economic and political factionalism, the postindependence government abolished these traditional units and reorganized the country into governorates (*muḥāfaẓāt*).

United Yemen eventually embraced a system based, as in South Yemen, on a series of governorates. The governorates are in turn divided into several hundred districts. The governors of the governorates are appointed by the federal president, but each jurisdiction has its own elected council. An important issue that remains to be resolved is the amount of authority that the governorates will have in the federal system. The trend in both the north and the south was to provide the governorates with a high degree of autonomy. The first municipal elections under the Local Authority Law (1999) were held in 2001. However, Yemen has lacked the infrastructural resources to conduct efficient local elections, and safeguards providing protection from the interference of the central government have been slow to materialize.

JUSTICE

The two parts of the new state had markedly contrasting legal traditions. In the north the legal system had been a mix of Sharīʿah (Islamic law) and *ʿurf* (tribal custom). In the south the legal system was a mixture of Sharīʿah in matters of personal status (e.g., marriage, divorce, inheritance) and British commercial and common law (modified to suit the needs of the Marxist government) and, in rural areas, a combination of Sharīʿah and *ʿurf*.

New legal codes were promulgated in 1991–94. Each district has a court of first instance, and each governorate has a court of appeals; the Supreme Court is located at the capital. These courts have full competency to hear all civil and criminal cases. The Supreme Judicial Council oversees the court system. There are a number of specialized courts. Under the constitution, Sharīʿah is the source of all legislation.

POLITICAL PROCESS

There are a number of active political parties at the national level, but the composition and membership of political parties are regulated by law. Parties based on such factors as regional, tribal, sectarian, or ethnic persuasion are expressly prohibited. Each party must seek a license from a state committee to legally exist. The most successful party by far is the General People's Congress. Other parties include Iṣlāḥ (the Yemeni Congregation for Reform), the Nasserite Unionist Party, and several socialist organizations.

SECURITY

The combined armed forces of Yemen, including army, air force, and navy, are small and poorly equipped by the standards of the region. Since the unification of the state in 1990, the manpower of Yemen's conventional army has suffered a general decline. The extensive inventories of Eastern-bloc weapons that the country inherited rapidly became dated, and many weapons systems were discarded. The military consists of volunteers serving two-year enlistments, and there is no consistent military educational or professional development system or enlisted personnel or officers. Military strength has been augmented by a large number of paramilitary forces, mostly associated with the Ministry of the Interior. Also, there are a relatively small number of reservists and tribal levies that the government can call on in times of emergency.

Military officers have often involved themselves in political affairs; in the north, the military played the dominant role in the political system following the overthrow of the civilian government by Col. Ibrāhīm al-Ḥamdī in 1974. Internal security is a major concern of the government. The Political Security Organization is the major intelligence organ of the state. Police and paramilitary groups provide security, and the Criminal Investigation Department conducts criminal investigations.

HEALTH AND WELFARE

In spite of the generally healthy climate of the Yemeni highlands, where most of the population live, the standard of public health remains very low. Contributing factors include: (1) unsanitary water supplies, (2) numerous cultural patterns that compromise both personal and group hygiene, (3) the presence of numerous diseases at endemic rates (e.g., malaria in the coastal belt and gastroenteritis in the highlands), (4) the very high birth rate, and (5) insufficient personnel and financial resources to provide modern medical care and to undertake any massive public health programs. There are various programs supported and operated by foreign donors that address these needs to some degree. Sanaa and Aden have numerous hospitals, but few meet Western standards of sanitation and medical practice.

HOUSING

Although Yemeni architecture is among the loveliest and most fascinating in the Arab world, housing stock in general tends to be of poor quality. There are two basic housing types: houses of reed, thatch, and mud brick, which are largely found in coastal regions; and houses of stone and mud brick, which are more frequently found in the highlands.

Throughout the country, access to fresh water and hygienic sewage disposal is poor. Houses with running

The mud brick multistory houses of Shibām, Yemen. Lynn Abercrombie

water, internal sewage systems, and electricity remain the exception in most parts of the country, particularly in rural areas, where only a small fraction have indoor plumbing.

EDUCATION

Modern systems of education were established in both Yemens during the 1960s, but limited resources and a high birth rate ensured that education continued to reach only a fraction of school-age children. For a variety of social and cultural reasons, certain subgroups of the school-age population—most notably girls—remained underrepresented in the system. In spite of the dramatic expansion of teacher training, the lack of adequately qualified Yemeni teachers was a major problem in the north; Egyptian and other Arab expatriates largely filled this void. The overall literacy rate remains relatively low, and the disparity between males and females is large. More than three-fourths of men and some two-fifths of women are literate. Partly because of an inadequate infrastructure that includes classroom shortages and poor materials and facilities, only a portion of eligible children enroll in school. Among those who do attend, only a small fraction go on to complete secondary education.

Higher education is limited to a very small minority. The University of Sanaa (founded 1970), established largely with grants from Kuwait, is coeducational and comprises a variety of specialized colleges—e.g., those of agriculture, medicine, commerce, and law. The University of Aden (1975) offers a similar array of specialties. These two senior institutions of higher learning have spawned universities and colleges throughout Yemen, and there are now several small colleges as well as vocational and polytechnic institutes in the larger urban centres that provide training in a variety of fields. However, wealthy families typically send their children abroad for higher education.

In addition, both of the major Muslim sects operate religious institutes for the preparation of judges and other religious personnel, although this often requires additional study at such well-known institutions as al-Azhar University in Cairo. By the carly 21st century the number of small religious schools associated with foreign Islamic groups had proliferated. Several thousand small religious academies were closed in 2005, and all non-Yemenis matriculating in unregistered schools were asked to leave the country for fear such institutions were involved in religious extremism.

CHAPTER 9

YEMENI CULTURAL LIFE

Yemen is a part of the Islamic world and as such reflects many of the contemporary trends in Islam. Most Yemenis are Muslim and are tolerant of non-Muslims as well as of the various branches of Islam. While proud of their Islamic heritage, Yemenis are also intensely proud of their pre-Islamic history, including that of the Saba' and Ḥaḍramawt kingdoms. In their extensive networks of overland and maritime trade, the ancient Yemenis encountered myriad cultures and civilizations. There is ample evidence of Greek, Roman, Indian, Indonesian, and Chinese influence on various aspects of both traditional and contemporary Yemeni culture.

DAILY LIFE AND SOCIAL CUSTOMS

Yemen shares in many of the customs and lifeways that are found in other parts of the Arab world. Culture is intensely patriarchal, and households usually consist of an extended family living in a single domicile or family compound. The head of the family is the eldest male, who makes all significant decisions for the family and its members. Women play a secondary role in running the household and raising the children and, in rural areas, helping to work the family farm. Though nearly one-fourth of Yemeni women obtain work outside the home, a woman traditionally earns most of her social status through bearing children, particularly males. The birth of a male child is considered one of the most important social events in Yemeni society and is followed almost immediately by a circumcision ceremony. Though prohibited by law in 2001, female genital cutting still occurs, taking place primarily in private and varying significantly by region.

Marriages are almost always arranged and frequently are undertaken at a young age. Although the opinion of a potential bride or groom might be solicited on the issue, the final decision on marriage belongs with the head of the household. As in many parts of the Islamic world, endogamy (the practice of marrying someone from within one's own kin group) is common, the preferred marriage being with a paternal first cousin of the opposite gender. The practice of *mahr* (bride-price, given by the father of the groom) is a usual part of the marriage ceremony. Divorce is not common, but neither is there a stigma attached to it. Men may have as many as four wives at the same time, though in practice it is rare for a man to take more than one wife.

Yemeni society is tribally based, and trust and assurance most often are measured by degree of consanguinity. Families are very close and are the focus of the individual's primary devotion. One's second allegiance is to the tribe, an extended family unit that ordinarily traces its ties to a common eponymous ancestor. In rural Yemen, state authority is weak, and disputes between tribes are frequently solved through violence. The art of the feud is still quite real, and, as a consequence, Yemen is a gun culture. Virtually every household has at least one weapon, and men and boys often carry firearms in public. Even when not carrying a pistol or a rifle, most Yemeni males—particularly those belonging to a rural tribe—will carry a dagger, the traditional *janbiyyah* (or *jambiyyah*), a short, broad, curved blade sheathed on a belt worn across the abdomen and serving as a signal of one's status within social and tribal hierarchies.

The traditional nature of Yemeni society is reflected in choices of attire, though the native dress of Yemen

A janbiyyah, *sheathed in the traditional fashion.* John Miles/The Image Bank/Getty Images

differs somewhat from that found in other conservative parts of the Arabian Peninsula. Men sometimes wear the full-length, loose-fitting *thawb*—frequently with a jacket over it—but more often the traditional *fūṭah*, a saronglike wraparound kilt, is worn with a shirt. The turban is a common type of head covering, and a finely woven bamboo hat (shaped somewhat like a fez) called a *kofiya* (or *kofia*) is a more formal choice of headgear.

There are various forms of dress for women, depending on the social role a woman plays and where she lives. In North Yemen, women in cities and towns wore the *sharsaf*, a black skirt, scarf, and veil ensemble that covers the entire body. In South Yemen, the regime that succeeded the British after 1967 vigorously opposed this women's dress code, and this opposition prevailed especially in the towns and cities. In the countryside, clothing for women tends to be somewhat more utilitarian and may consist of a dress or robe that provides for a greater range of movement and under which, in some parts of Yemen, it is not uncommon for a woman to wear a pair of loose slacks known as a *sirwāl*. Also in the countryside, a woman's face may or may not be covered, and dresses are sometimes sewn from brightly coloured fabric. Working women frequently wear a broad-brimmed straw hat (*dhola*) to ward off the sun.

Traditional Yemeni cuisine is broadly similar to that found in other areas of the Arabian Peninsula, but it is also heavily influenced by the cuisine of eastern Africa and South Asia. The major meats are chicken, mutton, and goat. Other staples include potatoes, onions, and tomatoes. There are several types of bread; unleavened flat bread is typical. A popular dish in Yemen is *saltah*, a stew of lamb or chicken that is heavily spiced with fenugreek and other herbs. Tea is a common drink, and coffee is very popular. Alcoholic beverages are considered culturally and religiously inappropriate, though they are available.

Unquestionably the most important and distinctive social institution and form of recreation in Yemen is the khat party, or khat "chew." This is especially true in the northern part of the country, but, since the slight increase in general prosperity in the 1970s, the use of khat has spread to virtually all levels of Yemeni society. At least half of all men, and a smaller number of women, attend khat chews (which usually are segregated by gender) with some regularity, and many do so on a daily basis. Khat chews usually begin in the early afternoon after the main meal of the day, and they often go on until the early evening. Much gets done at these pleasurable sessions. Gossip is exchanged, serious matters are discussed and debated, political and business decisions are made, business is transacted, disputes and grievances are settled, Yemeni history and lore are passed on, and music and poetry are played and recited.

Yemenis celebrate the traditional Islamic holidays, including ʿĪd al-Aḍḥā (marking the culmination of the hajj rites near Mecca) and ʿĪd al-Fiṭr (marking the end of Ramadan), as well as the Prophet Muhammad's birthday. Shīʿites observe ʿĀshūrāʾ (commemorating the death of al-Ḥusayn ibn ʿAlī, the Prophet's grandson). The Day of National Unity is May 22, the day on which, in 1990, North Yemen and South Yemen were officially united. A number of other civil and religious holidays also are observed.

THE ARTS

No doubt the best-known artifact of Yemeni culture is its domestic architecture, which dates back more than 2,000 years. In the mountainous interior, buildings are constructed of stone blocks and bricks, both baked and sun-dried. These buildings, housing extended families, rise to four to six stories, with highly decorated windows and other features designed to beautify them and emphasize their height. On the edge of the desert and in other regions where stone for construction is not abundant, multistoried houses are usually made of mud brick, with the various layers emphasized and often tinted. These structures have curving, sensuous lines. The city of Sanaa and the towns of Zabīd and Shibām are noted for their architecture, and each has been listed as a UNESCO World Heritage site.

The most widespread and traditional cultural outlet is oral, in the form of proverbs, popular stories, and poetry. Poems that deal with timeless themes such as love and death as well as with Yemeni history, biography, and Islamic themes and traditions are particularly prevalent. Yemen is an integral part of contemporary Arab trends in literature, political essays, and scholarly writing; Yemeni poets, past and present, are among the most esteemed in the Arab world. Among these are the great 10th-century poet and historian al-Hamdānī and such modern writers as novelist Zayd Muṭīʿ Dammāj, poet and political chronicler ʿAbd Allāh al-Baraddūnī, and the prolific poet ʿAbd al-Azīz al-Maqāliḥ. Similarly, the songs and singers of Yemen are highly respected, and some Yemeni instruments (such as the lutelike *qanbus*, or *ṭurbī*, now largely replaced by the *ʿūd*) and genres (such as *al-ghināʾ al-ṣanʿānī*, or Sanaani song) are quite unique.

Dances, performed with or without musical accompaniment, are a feature of weddings and other social occasions; these are performed by men and women separately. The male dances are often performed with the *janbiyyah* dagger.

Al-Hamdānī

(b. 893?, Sanaa, Yemen—d. c. 945?)

Al-Hamdānī was an Arab geographer, poet, grammarian, historian, and astronomer whose chief fame derives from his authoritative writings on South Arabian history and geography. From his literary production al-Hamdānī was known as the "tongue of South Arabia."

Most of al-Hamdānī's life was spent in Arabia itself. He was widely educated, and he traveled extensively, acquiring a broad knowledge of his country. He became involved in a number of political controversies. When he was imprisoned for one of them, his influence was sufficient to invoke a tribal rebellion in his behalf to secure his release.

His encyclopaedia *Al-Iklīl* ("The Crown") and his other writings are a major source of information on Arabia, providing a valuable anthology of South Arabian poetry as well as much genealogical, topographical, and historical information. "Al-Dāmighah" ("The Cleaving"), a *qaṣīdah*, is perhaps his most famous poem; in it he defends his own southern tribe, the Hamdān. It has been said that al-Hamdānī died in prison in Sanaa in 945, but this is now in question.

CULTURAL INSTITUTIONS

The General Organization of Antiquities and Museums administers the major cultural institutions. Most institutions are located in the larger cities. The national museum in Sanaa and the archaeological museum in Aden house important treasures from the pre-Islamic period. The Military Museum is located in Sanaa. There are also military and folk museums in Aden.

SPORTS AND RECREATION

Organized sports fall under the auspices of the Ministry of Youth and Sports. North Yemen first appeared in Summer

Yemini boxer Isra Girgrah (foreground, right) *during a 1997 bout at New York City's Madison Square Garden.* Al Bello/Getty Images

Olympic competition in 1984 and South Yemen in 1988; the unified country has sent teams to the Summer Games since 1992. Two Yemeni boxers living abroad enjoyed great success. Naseem Hamed, a British boxer of Yemeni ancestry, held the world featherweight title during the late 1990s and early 21st century. Isra Girgrah, a female boxer born in Yemen and fighting out of the United States, held several lightweight belts during that same period.

MEDIA AND PUBLISHING

Through its control of the media, education, and trade, the socialist government of the south severely restricted the participation of its population in both regional and global cultural trends during its most ascetic period, extending from the mid-1970s to the mid-1980s. The northern government correspondingly exercised certain restrictions in order to protect itself from the influence of the socialist south and from other challenges to the reigning political and cultural norms. In both Yemens, newspapers and magazines were closely censored, and radio and television were monopolized by the state.

These conditions changed drastically with the merger in 1990. Since that time, numerous newspapers and journals—representing divergent points of view and a wide range of political, social, economic, and cultural organizations—have come into being. The national television and radio networks, although still operated by the government, are less strictly controlled than before unification.

CHAPTER 10

YEMEN: PAST AND PRESENT

For more than two millennia prior to the arrival of Islam, Yemen was the home of a series of powerful and wealthy city-states and empires whose prosperity was largely based upon their control over the production of frankincense and myrrh (two of the most highly prized commodities of the ancient world) and their exclusive access to such non-Yemeni luxury commodities as various spices and condiments from southern Asia and ostrich plumes and ivory from eastern Africa. The three most famous and largest of these empires were the Minaean (Maʿīn), the Sabaean (Sabaʾ, the biblical Sheba), and the Ḥimyarite (Ḥimyar, called Homeritae by the Romans), all of which were known throughout the ancient Mediterranean world. Their periods of ascendancy overlap somewhat, extending from roughly 1200 BCE to 525 CE.

From its rise in the early 7th century CE, Islam spread readily and quickly in Yemen. The Prophet Muhammad sent his son-in-law as governor, and two of Yemen's most famous mosques—that in Janadiyyah (near Taʿizz) and the Great Mosque in Sanaa (said to have incorporated some materials from earlier Jewish and Christian structures)—are thought to be among the earliest examples of Islamic architecture.

For the history of Yemen, the most important event after the triumph of Islam was the introduction in the 9th century of the Zaydī sect from Iraq—a group of Shīʿites who accepted Zayd ibn ʿAlī, a direct descendant of Muhammad, as the last legitimate successor to the Prophet. Much of Yemeni culture and civilization for the next 1,000 years was to bear the stamp of Zaydī Islam. That same span of time was host to a confusing series of factional, dynastic, local, and imperial rulers contesting against one another

A scholar leads Yemeni students through their lessons amid the resplendent early architecture of the Great Mosque in Sanaa. Marwan Naamani/AFP/Getty Images

and against the Zaydīs for control of Yemen. Among them were the Ṣulayḥids and the Fāṭimids, who were Ismāʿīlīs (another Shīʿite branch); the Ayyūbids; and the Rasūlids, whose long rule (13th–15th century) firmly established Sunnism in southern and western Yemen.

Yemen next appeared on the world stage when, according to one account, the leader of a Sufi religious order discovered the stimulating properties of coffee as a beverage, probably about the beginning of the 15th century. As a result, Yemen and the Red Sea became an arena of conflict between the Egyptians, the Ottomans, and various European powers seeking control over the emerging market for *Coffea arabica* as well as over the long-standing trade in condiments and spices from the East; this conflict occupied most of the 16th and 17th centuries. By the beginning of the 18th century, however, the route between Europe and Asia around Africa had become the preferred one, and the world had once again lost interest in Yemen. In the meantime, the coffee plant had been smuggled out of Yemen and transplanted into a great variety of new and more-profitable locales, from Asia to the New World. The effect of the redirection of trade was dramatic. Cities such as Aden and Mocha (as the name would suggest, once a major coffee centre), which had burgeoned with populations in excess of 10,000, shrank to villages of a few hundred.

THE AGE OF IMPERIALISM

Developments in the 19th century were fateful for Yemen. The determination of various European powers to establish a presence in the Middle East elicited an equally firm determination in other powers to thwart such efforts. For Yemen, the most important participants in the drama were the British, who took over Aden in 1839, and the Ottoman Empire, which at mid-century moved back into North Yemen, from which it had been driven by the Yemenis two centuries earlier. The interests and activities of these two powers in the Red Sea basin and Yemen were substantially intensified by the opening of the Suez Canal in 1869 and the reemergence of the Red Sea route as the preferred passage between Europe and East Asia. As the Ottomans expanded inland and established themselves in Sanaa and Taʿizz, the British expanded north and east from Aden, eventually establishing protectorates over more than a dozen of the many local statelets. This was done more in the interest of protecting Aden's hinterland from the Ottomans and their Yemeni adversaries than out of any desire to add the territory and people there to the British Empire.

By the early 20th century the growing clashes between the British and the Ottomans along the undemarcated border posed a serious problem. In 1904 a joint commission surveyed the border, and a treaty was concluded, establishing the frontier between Ottoman North Yemen and the British possessions in South Yemen. Later, of course, both Yemens considered the treaty an egregious instance of non-Yemeni interference in domestic affairs.

The north became independent at the end of World War I in 1918, with the departure of the Ottoman forces. The imam of the Zaydīs, Yaḥyā Maḥmūd al-Mutawakkil, became the de facto ruler in the north by virtue of his lengthy campaign against the Ottoman presence in Yemen. In the 1920s Imam Yaḥyā sought to consolidate his hold on the country by working to bring the Shāfiʿī areas under his administrative jurisdiction and by suppressing much of the intertribal feuding and tribal opposition to the imamate. In an effort to enhance the effectiveness of his campaigns against the tribes and other fractious elements, the imam sent a group of Yemeni youth to Iraq in the mid-1930s to learn modern military techniques and weaponry. These students would eventually become the kernel of domestic opposition to Yaḥyā and his policies.

Yemeni independence allowed the imam to resuscitate Zaydī claims to "historic Yemen," which included Aden and the protectorate states, as well as an area farther north that had been occupied only recently by an expanding Kingdom of Saudi Arabia, including the province of Asir and some important areas around the Najrān oasis and Jīzān. These areas became a point of conflict with the house of Saʿūd. Yaḥyā, of course, did not recognize the standing Anglo-Ottoman border agreement.

The British, on the other hand, retained control over the south, which they considered strategically and economically important to their empire. Friction between the imamate and Britain characterized the entire interwar period, as Imam Yaḥyā sought to include the south in the united Yemen that he perceived to be his patrimony. The British in the meantime were consolidating their position in the south. The most important change was the incorporation of the Ḥaḍramawt and its great valley into the protectorate system—the result of the labours of British diplomat Harold Ingrams, who negotiated the famous "Ingrams's Peace" among the more than 1,400 tribes and clans that had been feuding in that district for decades.

By the end of World War II in 1945, dissatisfaction with Yaḥyā and his imamate had spread to a rather wide segment of Yemeni society, including both secular and Muslim reformers and modernists, other elements of the traditional elite, and even the ulama. This tide of dissent culminated in early 1948 in the assassination of Yaḥyā and a coup by a varied coalition of dissidents. Much to the consternation of the plotters, however, Yaḥyā's son Aḥmad succeeded in bringing together many of the tribal elements of the north, overthrew the new government, and installed himself as imam. Although Imam Aḥmad ibn Yaḥyā had indicated that he supported many of the popular political, economic, and social demands (e.g., creation of a cabinet with real responsibilities, abandonment of the principle of economic autarky, and the establishment of free public education), his own government soon resembled his father's in nearly all respects. An attempt on Aḥmad's life in 1955 only increased repression. Indeed, his paranoia concerning the loyalty of major tribal elements prompted actions that eventually cost his son tribal support during the civil war after the 1962 revolution.

In the meantime, the policies of both imams had backfired in the south. Although they had the advantage of offering an indigenous Muslim regime as an alternative to secular British rule, the imams' aggressive policies had alarmed many of the ruling families of the statelets in the south. The latter now believed, probably correctly, that, if their small statelets were to be taken over by the imam, their perquisites and status would be curtailed if not eliminated. Consequently, most deemed it advantageous to cooperate more closely with Britain, which, after all, subsidized them and implied a role for them in future arrangements. By the late 1950s an earlier proposal to federate some of the smaller statelets had grown into a much broader scheme to include all the principalities and sheikhdoms in a larger political entity that would eventually achieve independence.

Britain's insistence that Aden be a part of the new entity created the anomaly that eventually killed the plan. The sophisticated business community, the activist trade unions, and other similarly modern political and social organizations in Aden feared for their future at the hands of what they perceived to be a group of largely illiterate and parochial tribal leaders from the backward rural protectorates. The tribal leaders, on the other hand, feared at worst their overthrow or at best a degree of political and economic participation severely limited by an Adeni population that included some non-Muslims and many non-Arabs.

The British continued to insist upon their chosen course of action, and by 1965 all but 4 of the 21 protectorate states had joined the Federation of South Arabia. Shortly thereafter, Britain announced that it would leave southern Arabia and that independence would ensue no later than 1968. This announcement unleashed the violent political conflict that prevailed in Aden and the protectorates for the next two years as sundry organizations fought for control of the destiny of South Yemen.

Yaḥyā

(b. 1867, Yemen—d. Feb. 17, 1948, Sanaa, Yemen)

Yaḥyā Maḥmūd al-Mutawakkil was a Zaydī imam who succeeded in building a state in northern Yemen, which he ruled until his death in 1948.

When Yaḥyā was a child, Yemen was a province of the Ottoman Empire. His youth was spent in the service of his father's administration, and, when his father died in 1904, Yaḥyā succeeded him as imam. The Yemenis had always resented Turkish rule, and Yaḥyā was soon able to assemble a potent military force. Sporadic warfare lasted until 1911, when he was able to force the Turks to recognize the autonomy of his personal rule over the Yemen. He remained loyal to the Turks when World War I broke out but did not take an active part in the hostilities. At the close of the war he was recognized as the independent ruler of the Yemen, but there was no agreement on just which territories composed the country.

Yaḥyā clashed with the British, who had a military base in Aden and who considered many of the neighbouring tribes to be under their protection. He also clashed with his Arab neighbours along the Red Sea coast in the province of Asir. War with the Saudis broke out in 1934, just after the conclusion of the treaty with Great Britain, and Yaḥyā suffered a decisive defeat. Ibn Saʿūd was generous, forced the imam to make no territorial concessions, and permitted a reversion to the prewar status quo. Thereafter foreign affairs ceased to be a dominant concern, and Yaḥyā directed his attention mostly to stabilization at home.

The hallmark of his rule was isolation from the outside world. His military power was based on the support of the Zaydī tribesmen of the interior highlands, while he administered the country through a small class of nobles known as *sayyid*s. Yaḥyā himself secured what amounted to a monopoly of Yemen's foreign trade. He was most concerned that no foreign influences disrupt this delicate equilibrium. He received some economic and military aid from the Italians in the 1920s and '30s but firmly refused close contacts, such as an exchange of diplomatic missions. During World War II he remained neutral, but trouble began afterward, when the British strengthened their position in Aden and Yemenis who were discontented with Yaḥyā isolationist autocracy looked to them for support. Yemenis abroad also supported the domestic dissidents, but opposition did not become active until 1946. Two years later, the aged imam was assassinated.

TWO YEMENI STATES

In the north, meanwhile, Aḥmad died of natural causes in September 1962, and his son Muḥammad al-Badr became imam. Within a week, elements of the military, supported by a variety of political organizations, staged a coup and declared the foundation of the Yemen Arab Republic (North Yemen). The young imam escaped from his battered palace, fled into the northern highlands, and began the traditional process of rallying the tribes to his cause. The new republic called upon Egypt for assistance, and Egyptian troops and equipment arrived almost immediately to defend the new regime of ʿAbd Allāh al-Sallāl, the nominal leader of the 1962 revolution and the first president of North Yemen. Nearly as quickly, Saudi Arabia provided aid and sanctuary to the imam and his largely tribal royalist forces.

The establishment of a republic in North Yemen provided a tremendous incentive to the elements in the south that sought to eliminate the British presence there. Furthermore, the Egyptians agreed to provide support for some of the organizations campaigning for southern independence—e.g., the Front for the Liberation of (Occupied) South Yemen (FLOSY). However, not all elements in either of the two Yemens were sympathetic to

Egyptian policies, much less to the dominant role that Egypt had begun to play in southern Arabia. A new, radical alternative movement, the National Liberation Front (NLF), drew its support primarily from indigenous elements in the south. As the time for independence drew near, the conflict between the various groups, and especially between the NLF and FLOSY, escalated into open warfare for the right to govern after British withdrawal. By late 1967 the NLF clearly had the upper hand; the British finally accepted the inevitable and arranged the transfer of sovereignty to the NLF on Nov. 30, 1967.

The new government in Aden renamed the country the People's Republic of South Yemen. Short of resources and unable to obtain any significant amounts of aid, either from the Western states or from those in the Arab world, it began to drift toward the Soviet Union, which eagerly provided economic and technical assistance in hopes of bringing an Arab state into its political sphere. By the early 1970s South Yemen had become an avowedly Marxist state and had inaugurated a radical restructuring of the economy and society along communist lines, renaming itself the People's Democratic Republic of Yemen.

In North Yemen the conflict between the imam's royalist forces and the republicans had escalated into a full-blown civil war that continued fitfully and tragically until 1970. Participation, however, was not limited to the Yemenis. Saudi Arabia, Iran, and Jordan supported the royalists, whereas Egypt and the Soviet Union and other Eastern-bloc states supported the republicans. Britain and the United States, as well as the United Nations, also eventually became major players, even if only at the diplomatic level.

By the late 1960s, however, the Yemenis decided that the only logical outcome of the conflict was a compromise, which would have as its most important side effect the departure of the various foreign forces. Al-Sallāl's pro-Egyptian regime was ousted in a bloodless coup in 1968 and replaced by a nominally civilian one headed by Pres. ʿAbd al-Raḥmān al-Iryānī. Two years later, with the blessing of the two major foreign participants—Egypt and Saudi Arabia—the leaders of North Yemen agreed upon the Compromise of 1970, which established a republican government in which some major positions were assigned to members of the royalist faction. It was agreed that the imam and his family were not to return to Yemen or to play any role whatsoever in the new state; accordingly, the imam went into exile in Britain and died there in the late 1990s.

The compromise government embarked haltingly upon a program of political and economic development, with few resources and even fewer skilled personnel to implement the desired changes. Impatient, the military and some tribal elements dismissed the civilian cabinet in 1974 and replaced it with a military-led Command Council headed by Ibrāhīm al-Ḥamdī, who appointed a cabinet largely composed of technocrats. That government slowly but surely began to build a set of more-modern institutions and to implement the beginnings of a program of development—at the local as well as the national level. Not all sectors of the population, however, accepted the government's new powers and influence over traditional political, economic, and social relationships. A clear indication of this discontent was the assassination of two presidents in rapid succession (al-Ḥamdī in 1977 and, only eight months later, Aḥmad al-Ghashmī in 1978). The People's Constituent Assembly, which had been created somewhat earlier, selected Col. ʿAlī ʿAbd Allāh Ṣāliḥ as al-Ghashmī's successor.

In spite of early public skepticism and a serious coup attempt in late 1978, Ṣāliḥ managed to conciliate most factions, to improve relations with Yemen's neighbours, and to

ʿAlī ʿAbd Allāh Ṣāliḥ at the 2010 Arab Summit. Ṣāliḥ has been a central force in the country's political and economic development since he was named president of the newly unified Yemen in 1990. Joseph Eid/AFP/Getty Images

resume various programs of economic and political development and institutionalization. More firmly in power in the 1980s, he created the political organization that was to become known as his party, the General People's Congress (GPC), and steered Yemen into the age of oil.

Now that the two Yemens were independent, expectations rose in some quarters that there would be some form of unification, especially since both states publicly claimed to support the idea. Such was not forthcoming, however, the primary reason being the drastic divergence of political and socioeconomic orientations of the two regimes by the end of the 1960s. Whereas the north elected to remain a mixed but largely market economy and to retain ties with the West as well as with Saudi Arabia, the south began to move rapidly in a socialist direction under the leadership of the more radical wing of the NLF.

Political differences led to a brief border war between the two Yemens in 1972. Notwithstanding efforts by some Yemenis and by others to resolve these disputes—indeed, in spite of the first of two aborted agreements to unify—the basic conflicts appeared irreconcilable. The South Yemenis perceived their cause, that of Marxist transformation of the Arab political, economic, and social systems, to be in desperate need of direct action. In fact, South Yemen helped to instigate and fund a broad-based opposition movement in the north, the National Democratic Front, in the mid-1970s; elements of the leadership sanctioned the assassination of the North Yemeni president, al-Ghashmī, in 1978. At the same time, South Yemen supported other revolutionary organizations in the region, such as the Popular Front for the Liberation of Oman. The continuing friction between the two Yemens led to another brief but more serious border war in 1979; as in the previous case, that conflict was followed by a short-lived agreement to unify.

All the while, however, significant fissures—both ideological and practical—were opening in South Yemen within the ruling Yemen Socialist Party (YSP), the party that evolved out of the NLF. ʿAbd al-Fattāḥ Ismāʿīl was the major ideologue of the YSP, as well as head of state and the driving force behind South Yemen's move toward the Soviet Union earlier in the 1970s. Late in that decade, he was opposed by his former ally and leader of the "Chinese faction" in the regime, South Yemen president Sālim ʿAlī Rubayyī, whose visit to China inspired his politics with Maoist ideas. The conflict ended in Rubayyī's execution on charges that he had been behind the assassination of al-Ghashmī.

In turn, Ismāʿīl proved too dogmatic and rigid—in his analyses, policies, and methods of implementation—and was deposed in 1980. His successor, ʿAlī Nāṣir Muḥammad, instituted a far less dogmatic political and economic order. In January 1986 the various personal and ideological differences surfaced briefly in an episode of violent civil strife that left Ismāʿīl and many of his supporters dead, resulted in the exile of ʿAlī Nāṣir Muḥammad, and brought to power a group of moderate politicians and technocrats led by ʿAlī Sālim al-Bayḍ and Ḥaydar Abū Bakr al-ʿAṭṭas. It was this element of the YSP that undertook the negotiations that brought about the unity of the two Yemens. The ability of the new leadership to build popular political support and to revive the faltering development of South Yemen was tested in the late 1980s—and it was found wanting.

Unification of Yemen

Two factors made the unity agreement of 1990 possible. One was the discovery of oil and natural gas in both countries at roughly the same time and in roughly the same geographic region (from Maʾrib to Shabwah), some of which was in dispute between them (clearly, it would not have been in the best interest of either country to engage in a costly conflict over such important resources; it made far more sense to unite and share the profits to be gained from a rational exploitation of the deposits). The other deciding factor was the decision by Mikhail Gorbachev, then president of the Soviet Union, to abandon that country's support of the governments and policies of a number of eastern European states, some of which were South Yemen's principal sources of financial, technical, and personnel assistance. Once the communist bloc gave way to popular democratic movements, it was only a matter of time before the isolated South Yemeni regime would crumble. The rational option for the YSP—and the one it chose—was to enter into negotiations with North Yemen while still in power.

Inasmuch as the border wars of 1972 and 1979 each had concluded with unification agreements that, not surprisingly, were aborted in a matter of months, the decision by the two ruling parties in late November 1989 to unify the two states—and, more importantly, its actual implementation six months later—took many Yemenis and nearly all outside observers by surprise. Whereas South Yemen had taken the lead in the past, this effort to unify was initiated and pushed by the Ṣāliḥ regime of North Yemen. Adopted by the legislatures of the two Yemens on May 22, 1990, the constitution of the new republic was declared in effect on that date.

The final terms of unification called for the full merger of the two states and the creation of a political system based on multiparty democracy. Sanaa was declared the political capital, and Aden was to be the economic capital. After a 30-month transition period, elections of a new national legislature were to take place in November 1992 (although ultimately they would be postponed). During the transition period, the two existing legislatures would meet together as a single body, and all other offices and powers would be shared equally between the two ruling parties, the GPC and the YSP. Ṣāliḥ was to serve as interim president of the republic and al-Bayḍ, the secretary-general of the YSP, was to be vice president.

Efforts by the Ṣāliḥ government to strengthen and build support and legitimacy for the political system of united Yemen were sorely compromised by an environment marked by severe economic collapse and widespread deprivation, especially since these conditions came quickly after a period of improving economic conditions and soaring expectations. Most of the population in the northern part of Yemen had experienced better living conditions in the 1980s, if not before, and the prospects of oil revenues and the reputed benefits of unification had greatly raised expectations in both parts of Yemen at the end of the 1980s.

The indirect cause of the collapse of the Yemeni economy can be found in the Persian Gulf War (1990–91), which followed Iraq's invasion and occupation of Kuwait in August 1990. The growing importance of oil revenues notwithstanding, the Yemeni economy in the late 1980s remained heavily dependent on workers' remittances and external economic aid from Saudi Arabia and, to a lesser extent, the other oil-rich Persian Gulf states. In the fall of 1990, the newly created Republic of Yemen took the position that a diplomatic solution for Iraq's aggression should be reached between the Arab countries. Yemen's refusal to support the U.S.-Saudi military coalition against Iraq prompted Saudi Arabia to expel several hundred thousand Yemeni workers and to cut all foreign aid to Yemen; most of the other Arab oil states followed suit. Within months, the republic's GDP and government revenues—to which external aid contributed significantly—plunged; the unemployment and inflation rates, as well as the budget deficit, soared. By 1992, general contraction of the economy had produced widespread and deepening privation, and modest increases in oil revenues did not add much to the capacity of the new government to ease the growing suffering and to stem the collapse of the economy.

With the economy ailing, spats of political violence—including bombings and assassinations—marred the years leading to the republic's first general parliamentary elections. In spite of the growing acrimony, however, the unification regime was able to pull back from the political brink and hold the prescribed legislative elections in April 1993, only a few months later than originally planned; they were judged by international monitors to be relatively free and fair. President Ṣāliḥ's party, the GPC, emerged with a large plurality of seats. The Islamic Reform Grouping

(Iṣlāḥ), the main organized opposition to the unification regime since 1990, and the YSP both won strong minority representation. Holding virtually all the seats, the three parties formed a coalition government in May 1993, amid some hope that the political crisis had passed.

CIVIL WAR AND POLITICAL UNREST

Instead, the conflict between the northern and southern political leaders worsened dramatically in the second half of 1993 and the early months of 1994. For the second time in little more than a year, Vice President al-Bayḍ left Sanaa and retired to Aden, taking many of his YSP colleagues with him. In spite of major efforts at reconciliation, from within and without Yemen, the political struggle escalated into armed conflict in the spring of 1994, and YSP leaders and other southern politicians—still in control of their armed forces—resorted to armed secession in the early summer of that year. The War of Secession of 1994, lasting from May to early July, resulted in the defeat of the southern forces and the flight into exile of most of the YSP leaders and their soldiers and other supporters.

The short civil war left the YSP in political shambles and left control of the state in united Yemen in the hands of a GPC-Iṣlāḥ coalition dominated by President Ṣāliḥ. Over the next few years, the effort to reorganize politics and to strengthen the voice of the south in Yemen's political life was hampered in part by the inability of the YSP to resuscitate itself; at the same time, strained relations within the GPC-Iṣlāḥ coalition led to increasing dominance by the GPC and to an oppositional stance on Iṣlāḥ's part. The political conflict and unrest that accompanied and followed the civil war led to a revival of the power of the security forces and to the curtailment of the freedom of opposition parties, the media, and nongovernmental organizations. Human rights were being violated, but those violations were increasingly protested by groups within Yemen.

Yemen held its second parliamentary election on April 27, 1997. The GPC won a majority of the seats, Iṣlāḥ finished second, and the YSP virtually committed political suicide by boycotting the elections. Given its sizable majority, the GPC chose to rule alone, thereby making Iṣlāḥ the major opposition party in parliament. In late 1994 the plural executive had been abolished and President Ṣāliḥ reelected to a five-year term by parliament. In September 1999 he was again returned to office, this time in the country's first direct presidential elections and for a term lengthened to seven years. He had run virtually unopposed, as the YSP candidate was unable to secure the minimum number of votes necessary in the GPC-dominated parliament to stand in the election.

By late 1994 the economy of unified Yemen was in free fall, primarily the result of the loss of remittances and external aid after 1990 and, to a lesser extent, the costs of unification and the War of Secession. Rapidly increasing oil revenues notwithstanding, Yemen had ceased to be economically viable or sustainable. By 1995 it was clear to key leaders in the Ṣāliḥ regime that economic realities required greatly increased foreign investment and aid and that, in turn, these would not be forthcoming without a stabilized and restructured economy and a peaceful external environment.

Territorial Disputes

The Ṣāliḥ regime realized its undemarcated border with Saudi Arabia remained the major source of regional conflict—and even war—for Yemen. Thus the restoration of good relations with the Saudis and the resolution of the border issue were at the top of the Ṣāliḥ regime's foreign policy agenda. Its attention focused on its relations with the Saudis and the other oil-rich Persian Gulf states, the Ṣāliḥ regime was waylaid by a dispute in 1995 with newly independent Eritrea. At issue was possession of the Ḥanīsh Islands, a string of tiny islands in the Red Sea between the two countries. When Eritrea initiated conflict over Greater Ḥanīsh and captured Yemeni forces, the possibility of escalation into war became real. Yemen, concerned about frightening off investors, signed an agreement with Eritrea pledging to submit the dispute to international arbitration. In 1998 the arbitration board awarded most of the Ḥanīsh Islands to Yemen, and both sides accepted the ruling. Although relations between Yemen and Eritrea improved initially, they were often strained over the next decade.

The Eritrean conflict notwithstanding, relations with Saudi Arabia remained Yemen's primary external concern. Saudi pressure on Yemen's eastern border included threats to international oil companies working under agreements with Yemen in territory claimed by the Saudis. This pressure and a border clash in late 1994—the first of a string of such clashes over the next several years—spurred talks between Yemen and Saudi Arabia that led to the Memorandum of Understanding in January 1995. The agreement called for negotiations to finally determine the border and reaffirmed the Ṭāʾif treaty of 1934, which had both conditionally assigned the disputed territories of Asir, Najrān, and Jīzān to Saudi Arabia and confirmed the right of either country to resort to international arbitration if negotiations failed. After many rounds of talks and a Yemeni threat to resort to arbitration, in June 2000

Yemen and Saudi Arabia signed the long-sought final border agreement, increasing greatly the potential for friendly, mutually beneficial relations between the two countries. For Yemen, the major potential benefits were economic aid and the opportunity for Yemeni workers to once again seek employment in oil-rich Saudi Arabia.

Ḥanīsh Islands

The Ḥanīsh Islands (Arabic: Jazāʾir Ḥanīsh) form an archipelago in the southern Red Sea much of which, as of Nov. 1, 1998, was officially recognized as sovereign territory of Yemen. Long under Ottoman sovereignty, the island group's political status was purposely left indeterminate by the Treaty of Lausanne (1923), under which Turkey surrendered all its Asiatic territories outside Anatolia. Between 1923 and World War II, Italy exercised loose control over the fishermen frequenting the area. The islands were the subject of dispute and armed conflict between Yemen and Eritrea in late 1995 and 1996. Both countries agreed to accept arbitration, and in 1998 the Permanent Court of Arbitration ruled in favour of Yemen.

The four main islands of the Ḥanīsh group occupy a strategic position about 100 miles (160 km) north of the Strait of Mandeb, the southern entrance to the Red Sea. They extend from north to south in a chain about 40 miles (65 km) long and lie somewhat closer to Yemen than to Eritrea, between 20 to 45 miles (32–70 km) west of the Yemeni coast. From the north they are: Jabal Zuqar, the largest, which is irregularly shaped and about 10 miles (16 km) from north to south and 8 miles (13 km) from east to west at its widest point; Al-Ḥanīsh al-Ṣaghīr (Little Ḥanīsh); Al-Ḥanīsh al-Kabīr (Great Ḥanīsh); and Suyūl Ḥanīsh. Interspersed among these islands, and extending southwest to the coast of Eritrea, are many small islets and rocks; the group is a major navigational hazard of the southern Red Sea.

The island group is volcanic in origin and has rugged topography throughout. The island of Jabal Zuqar rises to 2,047 feet (624 m) above sea level; this is the highest elevation on any of the Red Sea's many islands. Although barren and inhospitable to settlement, the islands have rich fishing grounds. There are also indications of possible mineral and oil deposits around the islands.

ECONOMIC CHALLENGES

Faced with the economic collapse of a country whose GDP in 1995 was half that of 1990, the Ṣāliḥ regime addressed the economic situation with a sense of urgency. From 1995 through most of the first decade of the new millennium, the regime's efforts to restore the viability and sustainability of Yemen's economy turned largely on the ambitious, multistage IMF and World Bank package of reforms first agreed to by the Ṣāliḥ regime in 1995. The package consisted of a series of stabilization measures and major structural reforms—and the relevant governance reforms—that Yemen pledged to implement over the course of a decade in exchange for generous amounts of aid, both from those international bodies and from many other external sources. One major goal was to make Yemen an attractive target for much-needed foreign investment. Parallel (but secondary) to this was the effort to further exploit Yemen's limited oil resources and to begin taking advantage of its also-limited natural gas deposits.

The Ṣāliḥ regime successfully implemented the initial steps of the IMF and World Bank reform package over the last half of the 1990s. These included currency, budget, and trade reforms, all of which involved economic sacrifices to varying degrees by all sectors of the population. However, by the late 1990s the Ṣāliḥ regime demonstrated an increasing lack of will and capacity—mostly political capacity—to adopt and carry out the more demanding economic and governance measures in the package. As a result—and in spite of threats and some punitive actions by the IMF, the World Bank, and members of the donor community—little progress was made after 2000 in putting into place the reforms needed to attract investors to Yemen, create jobs, foster enterprise, and add to the GDP. In spite of gains in the second half of the 1990s, the economy soon plateaued at a low level and by 2005 was barely creating enough jobs and necessary public services to keep up with the country's rapid population growth. Unemployment remained high, as did the level of malnourishment and the proportion of the population living below the poverty line. As a result, Yemen's economic situation and prospects in the first decade of the 21st century were grim.

Behind the Ṣāliḥ regime's apparent lack of the will and capacity to do what was necessary for its survival was the very nature of that regime. In the 1980s the Ṣāliḥ regime in North Yemen had gradually crystallized into an oligarchy dominated by military officers, tribal sheikhs, and northern businessmen. Compromised somewhat by the politics of unification, this pyramid of patronage and privilege reasserted and extended itself after 1994; part of the extension involved the "occupation" of the south by northerners, especially military and security officers. Moreover, this "rule by the few" increasingly evolved into a special kind of oligarchy, a kleptocracy, in which the state—with only recent access to oil revenues and increased external aid—functioned primarily to enrich the oligarchs at the expense of the wider public. For the first time, the Yemeni state became a collection of profit centres for the rulers and their associates. Patronage, nepotism, bribery, fraud, and other corrupt practices became the norm rapidly and to an alarming degree.

YEMEN AND THE "WAR ON TERROR"

The nature and salience of Yemen's relations with many countries—but especially the United States—changed dramatically with al-Qaeda's terrorist attacks on the World Trade Center and the Pentagon on Sept. 11, 2001. In fact, the change in relations with the United States was anticipated in the reactions by both countries to the suicide bombing by al-Qaeda of a U.S. naval destroyer, the USS *Cole*, in Aden's port nearly a year earlier. Following U.S. embassy bombings in Kenya and Tanzania in 1998 and the rise of Islamic militants in nearby Somalia, the USS *Cole* incident brought the issue of militant Islam into relation with Yemen. President Ṣāliḥ's trip to Washington only days after the September 11 attacks to pledge Yemen's full support to U.S. President George W. Bush's "war on terror" notwithstanding, Ṣāliḥ thereafter had to balance the U.S. demand for no less than full support in the war against the realities of a domestic political landscape marked by Yemeni nationalism, strong Islamic sensibilities, growing anti-American sentiment, and—perhaps most importantly—the central role of some Yemeni militant Islamist leaders and groups in Yemen's domestic political balance of power. From the USS *Cole* bombing, and especially after the September 11 attacks, President Ṣāliḥ picked his way carefully, but imperfectly and with difficulty, between these often contradictory forces.

Yemen's link to revolutionary political Islam runs deeper than the USS *Cole* bombing and events in eastern Africa—or than the fact that the father of al-Qaeda founder Osama bin Laden immigrated to Saudi Arabia from Wadi Ḥaḍramawt in Yemen. Many of the recruits for the U.S.- and Saudi-orchestrated effort to mount a largely Islamic effort to oust the Soviet Union from Afghanistan in the 1980s came from Yemen, Saudi Arabia's neighbour. In the course of this effort, Afghanistan became the main incubator for this new phenomenon: global revolutionary Islam. When a collapsing Soviet Union withdrew from Afghanistan after 1989, trained and radicalized fighters from throughout the Islamic world made their way home. Specifically, many fighters—both Yemeni and non-Yemeni—went to Yemen, drawn by its porous borders and its vast tribal areas outside the control of the Yemeni state.

USS Cole *Attack*

On Oct. 12, 2000, Muslim militants associated with al-Qaeda attacked a U.S. naval destroyer, the USS *Cole*. Suicide bombers in a small boat steered their craft into the side of the USS *Cole*, which was preparing to refuel in the harbour in the Yemeni port of Aden; the blast ripped a 1,600-square-foot (150-square-metre) hole in its hull and left 17 sailors dead and 39 wounded.

In 2004 a Yemeni court tried Saudi-born ʿAbd al-Raḥīm al-Nashīrī in absentia for the USS *Cole* attacks and sentenced him to death; U.S. military prosecutors filed charges against him in 2008. The U.S. proceedings were complicated by the Central Intelligence Agency's (CIA's) admission that waterboarding—an interrogation tactic that simulates drowning, banned by the CIA in 2006—was used during Nashīrī's imprisonment at Guantánamo Bay; it was unclear whether evidence obtained through such means would be admissible in court.

A gaping hole in the port side of the USS Cole *is evidence of a terrorist attack on the ship while it was refueling in the Port of Aden in October 2000.* U.S. Navy/Getty Images

Thereafter, many of the Yemeni returnees, called "Afghan-Arabs," fought on the side of the Ṣāliḥ regime in the War of Secession in 1994. Indeed, the regime became indebted to some of them, and some developed close ties to the regime's topmost leaders.

In spite of both the domestic political problems posed by the war on terror and the unwillingness of the Yemeni oligarchs to adopt reforms that might restore economic viability and address the increasingly desperate condition of most Yemenis, the GPC engineered a big majority in the parliamentary elections in 2003. While Iṣlāḥ remained the only significant opposition party, the YSP did make something of a comeback. By this time, however, the YSP and Iṣlāḥ had joined with the Nasserites and two small Zaydī parties in an increasingly united and assertive opposition coalition, the Joint Meeting Parties (JMP). In 2006 President Ṣāliḥ again decisively won a new seven-year term, in spite of the relatively good showing by the candidate of the JMP; the GPC was also successful in the local council elections that were held at the same time. The JMP remained intact after the elections, maintaining a unified opposition to the Ṣāliḥ regime and at the same time planning for future elections.

MOUNTING CHALLENGE TO THE ṢĀLIḤ REGIME

The conflicting demands of the war on terror and the myriad problems facing Yemen's economy and society—and, in both areas, things done and left undone by the Ṣāliḥ regime—cumulatively increased resentment and dissatisfaction throughout Yemen in the first decade of the 21st century. The al-Ḥūthī (al-Houthi) Rebellion, launched in June 2004 in Ṣaʿdah in the far north by Zaydī sayyids who initially expressed their more general discontent by condemning the Ṣāliḥ regime as pro-American and pro-Israeli, resulted in many casualties over the next three months. In part as a result of the regime's heavy-handed response, the rebellion re-erupted in successive years and defied third-party efforts to reach a truce.

Beginning in mid-2007, an epidemic of protests and demonstrations, some of them violent, broke out over many months and in a large number of places across southern Yemen. Initiated by disgruntled military officers protesting their forced retirement and meagre pensions, these actions—and the regime's oftentimes harsh response—soon spread to civil servants, lawyers, teachers, professors, and unemployed youths protesting what they saw as the systematic discrimination against the south since the end of the War of Secession in 1994.

The rebellion in the north and the protests in the south evolved into questions of the legitimacy of the Ṣāliḥ regime, Yemeni unification, and even republicanism itself. Some protesting southerners, moving beyond the claim that unification amounted to occupation, openly began questioning again the notion of Yemeni unification. Even more crucially, some supporters of the al-Ḥūthī rebellion questioned republicanism itself and explicitly called for the restoration of the imamate and rule by Zaydī sayyids.

In addition, a number of bombings occurred in the diplomatic quarter of Sanaa in early 2008, at about the time that al-Qaeda called upon its Yemeni supporters to focus attacks on the western "crusaders" and their Yemeni allies. The bombing at the entrance of the U.S. embassy on September 17, in which some 16 people died, was only the worst of a string of violent incidents claimed by, or blamed on, al-Qaeda and its allies. The Ṣāliḥ regime's responses to this and other acts were swift and harsh. Thus, by the end of the first decade of the 21st century, the legitimacy and continuation of the Ṣāliḥ regime, and even Yemen itself, were being challenged in the north, east, south, and centre—in effect, from just about all quarters.

CONCLUSION

In many respects, Saudi Arabia and Yemen are opposites. With the world's largest oil reserves, Saudi Arabia is extremely wealthy. The country has been able to invest vast sums into developing its infrastructure, and consequently, literacy and life expectancy are relatively high and transportation and communication networks are good. By contrast, Yemen—likewise reliant upon oil, but possessing less and less of it—is among the world's more impoverished countries, and the provision of education, health care, and other infrastructural necessities is inadequate. Some 40 percent of Yemen's population is considered to be undernourished, compared with only 4 percent in Saudi Arabia. Saudi Arabia is overwhelmingly urban, while Yemen is almost as overwhelmingly rural. Although Saudi Arabia physically dominates the Arabian Peninsula and has a slightly higher population overall than its smaller and more densely populated neighbour, Saudi residents include a large number of expatriates—more than one-fourth of the country's population. Yemenis, in turn, have historically been more likely to work abroad.

In spite of such contrasts—and to some extent, because of them—events in Yemen and Saudi Arabia have long been closely linked. Sharing a lengthy and long-undemarcated border, Saudi Arabia and Yemen were often embroiled in boundary disputes. The Yemeni economy was highly reliant upon its wealthy neighbour. Numerous Yemeni labourers were employed in Saudi Arabia, and workers' remittances formed an especially important part of the Yemeni economy. Wary of the prospect of a powerful southern neighbour, Saudi Arabia was active in its efforts to prevent Yemeni unification—which was nevertheless achieved in 1990. Shortly thereafter, Yemen's intransigence during the Persian Gulf War led Saudi Arabia to expel Yemeni labourers wholesale, precipitating an economic crisis in Yemen that would have long-lasting effects. An agreement in 2000 that finally demarcated the border between the two countries helped to warm relations somewhat. More recently, though, violence associated with the al-Ḥūthī rebellion in northern Yemen, which has spilled into Saudi territory, has elicited a harsh response.

At the end of the first decade of the 21st century, the severity of the challenges facing Yemeni society—including the imminent depletion of oil and water resources and violent challenges to the Ṣāliḥ regime—meant that developments in Yemen would be closely watched. Some observers suggested the potential qualification of Yemen as a failed state, a prospect that ensured that events in that country would exert a powerful influence not only on Yemen's relationship with Saudi Arabia, but on regional stability on the whole.

GLOSSARY

autarky The state of being self-sufficient at the national level.

Bedouin Any member of a community of Arabic-speaking desert nomads of the Middle East.

dīwān An informal council in which a tribe's senior male hears outstanding grievances and dispenses justice.

endogamy The practice of marrying someone from within one's own kin group.

fūṭah A saronglike wraparound kilt traditionally worn by Yemeni men.

hajj A pilgrimage to the holy city of Mecca.

hegemony Having preponderant influence or authority over others.

imam The Muslim leader who leads prayers in a mosque.

janbiyyah A ceremonial dagger with a short, broad, curved blade that is sheathed on a belt worn across the abdomen.

kaffiyeh A traditional Arab headdress consisting of a square of cloth folded to form a triangle, which is held in place by a cord.

khat A slender, straight tree, the leaves of which are chewed for the stimulants they contain; the drug is central to social life in some countries, including Yemen.

madhhab A law school in Muslim countries that teaches jurisprudence from a religious (Islamic) point of view.

nomad Someone without a fixed residence, who moves from place to place within a well-defined territory.

oasis A stretch of desert land that contains a continual supply of fresh water.

oligarch One who believes that rule by a few is a proper form of government, particularly adhered to by those considered one of the few.

salt flat A salt-encrusted flat area resulting from evaporation of a former body of water.
sayyid An Arabic title of respect, restricted to members of Muhammad's clan.
sirwāl A pair of loose slacks worn by modern Yemeni women.
Sharīʿah Islamic law.
sharsaf A black skirt, scarf, and veil ensemble that covered the entire body, traditionally worn in northern Yemen.
sheikh The male head of each successive level of tribal social units, from the family and proceeding exponentially outward.
thawb The ankle-length shirt worn by Arab men, typically made from white cotton material.
ulama The most learned people of Islam.
ʿurf Law according to tribal custom.
xenophobia Exhibiting fear or hatred of all foreign people, places, or things.
xerophytic Requiring little water.
zakāt An obligatory alms tax levied on Muslims; one of the five Pillars of Islam.

BIBLIOGRAPHY

Overviews and general reference works on the land and people of Saudi Arabia include David E. Long, *The Kingdom of Saudi Arabia* (1997); and J.E. Peterson, *Historical Dictionary of Saudi Arabia* (1993). Mecca is the subject of F.E. Peters, *Mecca: A Literary History of the Muslim Holyland* (1994). An anthropological approach is taken in Soraya Altorki, *Women in Saudi Arabia: Ideology and Behavior Among the Elite* (1986). Also of importance is Donald Powell Cole, *Nomads of the Nomads: The Al Murrah Bedouin of the Empty Quarter* (1975, reissued 1988). Architecture and art are treated in G.R.D. King, *The Historical Mosques of Saudi Arabia* (1986), a study of mosque architecture; and Safeya Binzagr, *Saudi Arabia: An Artist's View of the Past* (1979), a pictorial perspective of Saudi Arabia's culture and people.

The economy of Saudi Arabia is examined in Ali D. Johany, Michel Berne, and J. Wilson Mixon, Jr., *The Saudi Arabian Economy* (1986); A. Reza S. Islami and Rostam Mehraban Kavoussi, *The Political Economy of Saudi Arabia* (1984); John R. Presley, *A Guide to the Saudi Arabian Economy*, 2nd ed. (1989); Arthur N. Young, *Saudi Arabia: The Making of a Financial Giant* (1983), a historical survey of the impact of oil; and Fouad Al-Farsy, *Saudi Arabia: A Case Study in Development*, rev. and updated (1989). Policy studies are found in Ragaei El Mallakh, *Saudi Arabia, Rush to Development: Profile of an Energy Economy and Investment* (1982); Hassan Hamza Hajrah, *Public Land Distribution in Saudi Arabia* (1982), on transformation of land ownership; and William B. Quandt, *Saudi Arabia in the 1980s: Foreign Policy, Security, and Oil* (1981), a diplomatic study. A more recent study of Saudi oil policy is Nawaf E. Obaid, *The Oil Kingdom at 100: Petroleum Policymaking in Saudi Arabia*

(2000). Further bibliographic information can be found in Hans-Jürgen Philipp, *Saudi Arabia: Bibliography on Society, Politics, Economics* (1984), in English and German; and Frank A. Clements, *Saudi Arabia*, rev. ed. (1988).

Defense issues are well covered in Nadav Safran, *Saudi Arabia: The Ceaseless Quest for Security* (1985, reissued 1988); and Anthony H. Cordesman, *Saudi Arabia: Guarding the Desert Kingdom* (1997).

Useful works on Saudi cultural life include Suraiya Faroqhi, *Pilgrims and Sultans: The Hajj Under the Ottomans, 1517–1683* (1994), which covers the history of the hajj in the 16th and 17th centuries. The pilgrimage as reflected in literature is very well presented in F.E. Peters, *The Hajj: The Muslim Pilgrimage to Mecca and the Holy Places* (1994). Politics and society in the home of the hajj, Mecca, in the 18th and early 19th centuries are admirably covered in William Ochsenwald, *Religion, Society, and the State in Arabia: The Hijaz Under Ottoman Control, 1840–1908* (1984).

Women's literature is the focus of Saddeka Arebi, *Women and Words in Saudi Arabia: The Politics of Literary Discourse* (1994). A historical approach to women in the kingdom is taken in Eleanor Abdella Doumato, *Getting God's Ear: Women, Islam, and Healing in Saudi Arabia and the Gulf* (2000).

Important historical works include Kamal Salibi, *A History of Arabia* (1980); and H.St.J.B. Philby, *Sa'ūdi Arabia* (1955, reprinted 1972). R. Bayly Winder, *Saudi Arabia in the Nineteenth Century* (1965, reprinted 1980), remains the definitive work on that period. The life of Ibn Sa'ūd, the founder of the modern Saudi state, is discussed in Mohammed Almana, *Arabia Unified: A Portrait of Ibn Saud*, rev. ed. (1982). Other treatments include David Holden and Richard Johns, *The House of Saud* (1981), a detailed history of the years 1902–80; and Ameen Rihani, *Ibn Sa'oud of Arabia: His People and His Land* (1928, reprinted 1983). Early Saudi foreign relations are discussed in Jacob Goldberg, *The Foreign Policy of Saudi Arabia: The Formative Years, 1902–1918* (1986). Works covering the same time include Madawi Al Rasheed, *Politics in an Arabian Oasis: The Rashidi Tribal Dynasty* (1991); Joshua Teitelbaum, *The Rise and Fall of the Hashimite Kingdom of Arabia* (2001); and Clive Leatherdale, *Britain and Saudi Arabia, 1925–1939: The Imperial Oasis* (1983). Joseph Kostiner, *The Making of Saudi Arabia, 1916–1936: From Chieftaincy to Monarchical State* (1993) is the best scholarly discussion of the kingdom's formative years. The kingdom in the reigns of Saʿūd and Fayṣ al is covered in Sarah Yizraeli, *The Remaking of Saudi Arabia* (1997), which follows Kostiner's approach. Histories of Aramco and U.S.-Saudi foreign policy include Irvine H. Anderson, *Aramco, the United States, and Saudi Arabia: A Study of the Dynamics of Foreign Oil Policy, 1933–1950* (1981); Aaron David Miller, *Search for Security: Saudi Arabian Oil and American Foreign Policy, 1939–1949* (1980); and Robert Vitalis, *America's Kingdom: Mythmaking on the Saudi Oil Frontier* (2006). Important studies of Saudi politics and Saudi-U.S. relations since the terrorist attacks of Sept. 11, 2001 include Dore Gold, *Hatred's Kingdom: How Saudi Arabia Supports the New Global Terrorism* (2003); Rachel Bronson, *Thicker than Oil: America's Uneasy Partnership with Saudi Arabia* (2006); and Thomas Lippman, *Inside the Mirage: America's Fragile Partnership with Saudi Arabia* (2004). Two important internal issues in the post-World War II period are analyzed in Ayman Al-Yassini, *Religion and State in the Kingdom of Saudi Arabia* (1985); and Alexander Bligh, *From Prince to King: Royal Succession in the House of Saud in the Twentieth Century* (1984). A later study of the succession is Simon Henderson, *After King*

Fahd: Succession in Saudi Arabia, 2nd ed. (1995). More on internal issues, such as political dissent, can be found in Mordechai Abir, *Saudi Arabia: Government, Society, and the Gulf Crisis* (1993); Mamoun Fandy, *Saudi Arabia and the Politics of Dissent* (1999); and Joshua Teitelbaum, *Holier than Thou: Saudi Arabia's Islamic Opposition* (2000).

A good general overview of Yemen is provided by Daniel McLaughlin, *Yemen* (2008), a Bradt Travel Guide. For would-be travelers or field researchers, Tim Mackintosh-Smith, *Yemen: Travels in Dictionary Land* (1997, reissued 2007); and Steven C. Caton, *Yemen Chronicle: An Anthropology of War and Mediation* (2005), are useful.

Various aspects of Yemeni culture and society are studied in Tomas Gerholm, *Market, Mosque, and Mafrag: Social Inequality in a Yemeni Town* (1997); Thomas B. Stevenson, *Social Change in a Yemeni Highlands Town* (1985); Charles F. Swagman, *Development and Change in Highland Yemen* (1988); Paul Dresch, *Tribes, Government, and History in Yemen* (1989); D. Brian Doe (ed.), *Socotra: Island of Tranquility* (1992); Martha Mundy, *Domestic Government: Kinship, Community, and Polity in North Yemen* (1995); Linda Boxberger, *On the Edge of Empire: Hadhramawt, Emigration, and the Indian Ocean, 1880s-1930s* (2002); and Shelagh Weir, *A Tribal Order: Politics and Law in the Mountains of Yemen* (2007). Studies focusing specifically on the use of khat in Yemen include John G. Kennedy, *The Flower of Paradise* (1987); and Shelagh Weir, *Qat in Yemen: Consumption and Social Change* (1985). Useful studies focused on migrants and migration include Jonathan Friedlander and Ron Kelley (eds.), *Sojourners and Settlers: The Yemeni Immigrant Experience* (1988); Fred Halliday, *Arabs in Exile: Yemeni Migrants in Urban Britain* (1992); and Enseng Ho, *The Graves of Tarim: Genealogy and Mobility Across the Indian Ocean* (2006).

For details on Yemeni art, architecture, and archaeology, useful works include R.B. Serjeant and Ronald Lewcock (eds.), *Ṣan'ā': An Arabian Islamic City* (1983); Steven C. Caton, *"Peaks of Yemen I Summon": Poetry as Cultural Practice in a North Yemeni Tribe* (1990); Brinkley Messick, *The Calligraphic State: Textual Domination and History in a Muslim Society* (1993); and Selma Al-Radi, *The 'Amiriya in Rada': The History and Restoration of a Sixteenth-Century Madrasa in the Yemen*, ed. by Robert Hillenbrand (1997).

Modern political analyses include Sheila Carapico, *Civil Society in Yemen: The Political Economy of Activism in Modern Arabia* (1998); Janine A. Clark, *Islam, Charity and Activism: Middle-Class Networks and Social Welfare in Egypt, Jordan and Yemen* (2004); Jillian Schwedler, *Faith in Moderation: Islamist Parties in Jordan and Yemen* (2006); and Sarah Phillips, *Yemen's Democracy Experiment in Regional Perspective: Patronage and Pluralized Authoritarianism* (2008). Useful studies on Yemeni international relations are Fred Halliday, *Revolution and Foreign Policy: The Case of South Yemen, 1967–1987* (1990); F. Gregory Gause III, *Saudi-Yemeni Relations: Domestic Structures and Foreign Influences* (1990); and Stephen Page, *The Soviet Union and the Yemens: Influence on Asymmetrical Relationships* (1985).

Encyclopaedic and bibliographic works include Robert D. Burrowes, *Historical Dictionary of Yemen*, 2nd ed. (2009); and Thomas B. Stevenson, *Studies on Yemen, 1975-1990: A Bibliography of European-Language Sources for Social Scientists* (1994).

Works on modern history, including politics and development, are Eric Macro, *Yemen and the Western World, Since 1571* (1968); Robert W. Stookey, *South Yemen, a Marxist Republic in Arabia* (1982), and *Yemen: The Politics of the Yemen Arab Republic* (1978); Manfred W. Wenner, *Modern Yemen,*

1918-1966 (1967), and *The Yemen Arab Republic: Development and Change in an Ancient Land* (1991); Robert D. Burrowes, *The Yemen Arab Republic: The Politics of Development, 1962–1986* (1987); Tareq Y. Ismael and Jacqueline S. Ismael, *The People's Democratic Republic of Yemen: Politics, Economics, and Society* (1986); Robin Bidwell, *The Two Yemens* (1983); B.R. Pridham (ed.), *Economy, Society & Culture in Contemporary Yemen* (1985), and *Contemporary Yemen: Politics and Historical Background* (1984); Jamal S. al-Suwaida (ed.), *The Yemeni War of 1994: Causes and Consequences* (1995); and Paul Dresch, *A History of Modern Yemen* (2000).

INDEX

F

G

H

I

J

K

L

M

N

O

P

Q

R

S

T

U

W

Y

Z